£3⁵⁰

Spiritual Fathers

*Restoring the
Reproductive Church*

Dan Schaffer

© 2006 by Building Brothers
11757 W. Ken Caryl Avenue, #F
PMB-337
Littleton, Colorado, 80127
www.buildingbrothers.org

Printed in the United States of America

ISBN: 0-9774478-0-4

Library of Congress Control Number: 2005937168

"Dan Schaffer knows the heart of men, and knows how to help the church become more effective with men. In plain and powerful language, this book is a blueprint for enabling the church to reach more men, and change men into the likeness of Christ. Dan hits the long ball when he teaches on the difference between churches as "production factories" versus *spiritual reproduction* that occurs when authentic disciples pass God's DNA to others. The latter is truly the key to the next great awakening of Christianity."

Larry Malone, Director, United Methodist Men Ministries

"I have journeyed with Dan for the past 15 years. Dan was one of the four founders of Promise Keepers in 1991. He is a man of integrity, a linear thinker and a man of vision. I love Dan Schaffer, support the ministry of Building Brothers and feel that his insight into men's ministry can benefit not only men, but the entire Church of Jesus Christ. Every pastor and leader would benefit from reading this clear presentation of the process that needs to be undertaken to pioneer a pathway to build spiritual fathers and ultimately impact our culture for Christ."

Dave Wardell, PhD, Co-Founder Promise Keepers

"Few men have the clear understanding of need for spiritual fathering that God has given Dan Schaffer. If you are a pastor or men's ministry leader, *Spiritual Fathers* is not an optional resource. Over the years, there have been several very good books for men. Yet, only a rare few are able to touch the very heart of what God is calling men to become and share with clarity the pathway to get them there. This book will become one of the benchmark books in men's ministry for years to come."

Dr. Chuck Stecker, President/Founder, A Chosen Generation

"Brilliant! From his wealth of experience in ministry to men and sensitivity to the Spirit, Dan Schaffer pin points a key issue in the Church today and lays out an effective plan to help the local church develop strong male leadership that will reproduce the passionate pursuit of God in the lives of others. These are not unproven ideas. Building Brothers has impacted men of our church. Building Brothers is not a course, not a class – but an *experience*! It is not a program. It is a transformational *process* that is building our men into spiritual fathers that we believe will "reproduce spiritual heirs." It is a *journey*. It is providing a pathway for our men to fulfill the vision and fourfold mission of our church.   I do believe the strength of the <u>process</u> is the secret...that it is not a program! It is life changing."

John Gordon, Pastor, Grace Chapel, Englewood, CO

"Finally!! A men's ministry tool that focuses on quality not just quantity. Many books tell how to build a men's ministry but few tell how to build the men along with the ministry. If you are serious about building godly men with depth, then this is the book for your ministry. Schaeffer's book is a must read for anyone serious about building men into spiritual anchors in the church."

Dr. Rod Cooper, Kenneth and Jean Hansen Professor of Discipleship and Leadership, Gordon-Conwell Theological Seminary

"The church is losing her men. The church desperately needs her men. How do we as leaders and shepherds in the body of Christ stem the tide of this troubling trend?   I don't have all the answers, but I know someone does. Do yourself and the men of your congregation a favor and read Dan Schaffer's book, *Building Spiritual Fathers*. He will answer the question 'of why men are so vital'... and what to do about it."

H.B. London, Jr., Vice President, Church, Clergy and Medical Outreach, Focus on the Family

Acknowledgements

Throughout my life countless men have spoke into me, challenged me and modeled the passionate pursuit of God for me. There is no way for me to name even a fraction of the men and women God used to shape me in preparation for this book. In the most recent years I have observed and journeyed with men building men all across the country and in Europe. I experienced God's heart to build men into mature spiritual fathers. Thank you, each and every one of you that God used to form this message.

I would like to give special thanks to the Building Brothers team. Rick Ellsmore, Dan'l Hollis and Ken Moldenhauer, helped guard and contribute to the purity, clarity and completeness of this message.

I would also like to thank Fran Taylor who helped us early in the editing process and Andrew Sloan who edited *Spiritual Fathers* into book form.

Lastly, I would like to extend a very special thanks to my wife Jan, my son Joel and my daughter Deb, who sacrificed, allowed and encouraged their husband and father to minister to men for the last 30 plus years. *Without them this book would have never happened.*

Dan Schaffer

Contents

Foreword

Here is a book that needs to be read, studied and used to help bring dynamic renewal to your church. It will take you to a very important beginning point that coincides with God's plan as unfolded in the biblical story. Developing godly men who serve as father figures is the key—a scriptural emphasis that never downplays the role of godly women but, in reality, elevates them to their God-ordained role to walk alongside us and help us become the leaders in the church, in our families and in our marriages that we are supposed to be.

My good friend and brother in Christ, Dan Schaffer, has outlined a process—not a program—that is intensely biblical as well as culturally relevant. He shares out of actual experiences serving men—from being one of the founding fathers of Promise Keepers to sharing this process in diverse cultural and ethical settings. His illustrations are powerful and illuminating and in touch with reality. In my opinion, his ecclesiology (his view of the church) is very perceptive and in harmony with the New Testament.

As pastors, we need to listen and learn from a "man in the pew" but also from a dynamic leader of men. Be warned, however! As a senior pastor particularly, you'll discover that you are the key—again not to a program, but to a process. Please don't let that frighten you. As a senior pastor, many "program oriented" leaders have told me their "programs" won't work without me. I always resisted that pitch. But tell me I'm a key to a biblical process that touches everything the church is about—now that gets my attention! I hope it will get yours too!

Dr. Gene A. Getz
Pastor Emeritus, Fellowship Bible Church North
President, Center for Church Renewal, Plano, TX

Preface
Do You Want Spiritually Alive Men?

If the church is to significantly impact society and experience lasting growth, it is vital that we as leaders help our men transform their lives, mature in Christ and become spiritual fathers who then reproduce spiritual fathers.

Do You, as a Pastor or Leader, Want Transformed Men?

For men to experience a spiritual life change and become *transformed*, the church must meet two primary needs: a *pathway* to spiritual maturity and a *transformational process* that offers a *safe masculine environment* where men can overcome the obstacles that keep them from pursuing God. Every church needs to provide this pathway where men are being healed alongside other men and being freed from the wounds of the past that control their lives. This pathway must help them to open up, trust and unite with other Christian brothers as they develop a new identity in Christ. A foundational issue that must be addressed in this transformational process is what we call the *father vacuum*—that is, dealing with the impact and influence our natural fathers have had on our lives. Most men are limited and restricted in how they view God; they see and relate to him in the way they have experienced their natural father. The Building Brothers transformation process will allow your men to experience God's blessing and approval and healing. They are then free to develop a renewed spiritual passion for a deeper relationship with Christ and their families, and to make a greater contribution to their communities.

Do You Want Spiritually Motivated Men?

Most pastors desperately want spiritually alive men who desire a deeper relationship with God—men who have fervor to truly know, worship and serve their Savior and the church! How do we move men from being pew warmers to a place of engagement with God and the church? How do we call men to the Great Commandment of loving God with all their heart, mind and strength and then to the Great Commission of building this love into other men? We help them experience an authentic and intimate relationship with God, free from their historical framework of the church being a performance-based religion where men serve God and the church out of *obligation* and miss the joy of serving from relationship and *opportunity*.

Do You Want Men with a Purpose?

The local church needs to become the place where men truly find their identity in Christ. They need to see the incredible opportunity to know their heavenly Father and co-labor with him as his son. When a man understands his true purpose, he passionately pursues God and allows God's love to grow within him and be poured into his family and community. These men will become directed and driven to *continue in the process of transformation and move out of patterns of obligation into experiences of opportunity to know and serve God.*

Do You Want Men Who Are Involved and Making an Impact?

We need men who have an enthusiasm to pursue God and make an impact as they journey daily with him. They know the importance of investing in eternal issues. These men are becoming *servant leaders* who understand the spiritual warfare around them and who, together with their Christian brothers, are willing to stay in that battle! This only happens when men are on a well-defined pathway to spiritual growth and maturity. On this pathway they discover Christ's model for *servant leadership* and catch his heart for love, unity and reconciliation among God's people. The men move forward, grounded and growing in the Great Commandment of loving God and then press into the Great Commission of reaching out to others.

Do You Want Men Who Experience Significance?

All men desire to have significance! Spiritually mature men desire to have *eternal* significance. They want to know that their lives truly counted for something permanent. For a godly man, this boils down to becoming a *spiritual father* who is in the process of reproducing *spiritual children* who in turn become *spiritual fathers* themselves. These men live out their lives as models and guides who are able to invite and influence other men to join them in spiritual realities they have personally experienced.

Do You Want Men Who Develop a Christ-like Lifestyle?

Men need a pathway that will lead them to become the spiritual head of their home, loving husbands and caring fathers, as well as to have a passion to serve the church. These men will also be known as contributing employees/employers and generous givers of time and resources to their communities.

What Is the Uniqueness of Building Brothers?

- Building Brothers is called *to serve the church*; it is not a "men's ministry" that pulls men out of the church.
- Building Brothers offers churches a *transformation process* for their men—not a short-term program or quick fix.
- Building Brothers helps church leaders create a *pathway for building spiritual maturity* in their men—not "five steps to success."
- Building Brothers helps in developing a *safe masculine pathway* where men process through the *root issues and obstacles that prevent them from pursuing intimacy with God*—without hype or pop psychology.
- Building Brothers assists in creating *servant leaders* who are trustworthy and will build unity within the church and its men, as opposed to leaders who lord over others by controlling or manipulating.
- Building Brothers partners with church leaders, not in an effort to generate programs and productions, but rather to build *spiritual fathers* who are then able to "reproduce" spiritual fathers and build a lasting legacy.

What Is Spiritual Fathering?

In the early 1970s I began to have a spiritual passion for pursuing God and reproducing that pursuit in others; this is commonly called discipling. I have been involved in the process of discipleship since that time.

A few years into this emerging calling I owned a business that was located in a Denver business complex. Some of the construction workers who worked at this complex told the younger men who worked with them to stay away from the "weird and dangerous guy who sits under the tree and reads his Bible." Well, that probably was a huge factor in one of those young men, Roger, not being about to stay away from me. Young men love danger!

Roger accepted Christ into his life and we started meeting daily over lunch. We spent many hours sitting under that tree digging deeper into the Word and God's plan for Roger's life. We both asked a lot of questions and we explored the answers together. This was an incredible time of pouring the life of Christ into Roger and seeing amazing changes in his life, in his values and perspectives and in his goals as a man. I remember him having a strong desire to see his seven siblings experience this new relationship that he had with Jesus Christ. (God honored this desire through the ensuing years.) Interestingly, the construction workers thought I was even more of a "Bible thumper" after my time spent with Roger.

Not long after this, Roger moved to Oklahoma to pursue a new job opportunity. There he met his wife and started a family. Each time Roger visited Denver he would connect with me; it was amazing how our relationship would pick up exactly where it left off. After five years Roger returned to Denver, and he and I started to meet regularly. His brother and a number of young men from varied backgrounds and denominations joined us once a week at 6 a.m. We continued to meet as a group for ten years.

Almost on a weekly basis, their lives and experiences brought up issues that they were facing as young men. We would go to different books of the Bible to specifically address their questions and apply the truth of God's Word to help shape their lives. They were remarkably open, freely exposing areas to the group that had not been exposed to other men in their lives.

I remember them asking, "Who is Jesus Christ?" We went to the Gospel of John to answer this vital question. They asked what it looked like to live the Christian life, and we looked deeper into the life of Daniel and David in the Old Testament. In this safe masculine environment, struggles with sex, pornography, marriage, children, money, work, anger, significance, commitment, obedience and most every other issue that men face came to the surface.

One day as our meeting was ending, Roger emphatically said, "You can say things to me that no one else could without making me angry." To further understand, I asked him, "Why is that?" He quickly responded, "I think it is because I know that you love me." This relationship was in the context of a safe environment that allowed openness, honesty and growth. It was the power of God's Spirit and the truth of his Word that brought about transformation.

Roger and I have been in relationship for over thirty years now. I was involved in his life when he married his lovely bride. I was there to see him raise his two sons, who are now committed followers of Christ. I will be there when grandchildren enter his life.

In the 1990s my schedule became so busy that we could no longer meet weekly. But we have continued in regular contact, and I have the opportunity to encourage and affirm Roger. I recently heard Roger share his perspective on our many years together:

> Dan is my earthly spiritual connection with my Father-God. Through the years Dan has become an integral part of my spiritual foundation as a man, and no other man on earth is as close to me as Dan. I've seen our sons grow up together; I remember the times that Dan served as a spiritual grandfather to my kids, mostly through the stories and lessons of life he imparted to them. I believe the strength of our relationship as men has been a tremendous witness to my kids as they've become adults. I can clearly see that God used my relationship with Dan as a model of hope and encouragement for me to build into the lives of men God has placed in my life. The most important "life lesson" I've learned from Dan was that our spiritual walk is a process—like Job, we have to go through the "school of hard knocks" to get to where God wants us to go. Our challenge as men is to stay in the battle.

The Promise Keepers Years

Even though I had been working with men for twenty years, it was during my time at Promise Keepers that God revealed the elements of his process of transforming men.

The first element that I saw was what I have come to call the **masculine context**. This is the safe male environment that allows men to open their hearts and be vulnerable with other men and God; this is what I had experienced in the years that I had been meeting with men. The masculine context allowed men to feel safe enough to let the Spirit of God lead them into a process of transformation.

The second element I discovered while at Promise Keepers was the father vacuum. The **father vacuum** is a hole in men's hearts as a result of the wounds left by their fathers. When we are threatened or hurt, we question our value and competence. This vacuum—a space devoid of anything—is always trying to fill itself with something. Many of us try to fill it with things that stroke our egos and make us feel worthy and valuable. The void makes us susceptible to addictive behaviors, so we are drawn to alcohol, drugs, sex, work, power, money, etc.

I remember meeting with a group of men while on a Promise Keepers trip to Nebraska in 1995 and 1996 where a young man, with tears running down his face, looked at me and said, "Thank you for causing mature men to accept and verbally affirm me." I was beginning to understand the need to allow other men to be used by God to help heal and fill the father vacuum with the love and acceptance of the Father God. I found that if this vacuum was not filled it was almost impossible to move toward pursuing God and knowing him intimately.

The third element I found that the church needed was Christ-like **servant leaders**: trustworthy pastors and other leaders who could lead the men of the church into the pursuit of God. I saw the positive impact on the church when leaders earned the right to be trusted and men could follow them into the pursuit of Christ. In contrast, when men did not trust their leaders they were unwilling to follow them anywhere.

And lastly, I believe our goal should be to **pursue and know God intimately**. When we possess God's spiritual DNA, he can use us to reproduce, building that pursuit in others.

I found that most of the major pieces were now in place to call men to a specific process or pathway that would take them from spiritual immaturity to maturity. I discovered that the full understanding of the mechanism and focus of that pathway was still missing. It wasn't until I started Building Brothers and journeyed for about three years that the rest of the picture started to become clear. I saw that God was calling his people to become spiritual reproducers, and only those men who understood that they were to be **spiritual fathers** would fully carry out their destiny and reproduce committed followers of Christ.

I want to challenge you to read on and see the power and impact that reproducing spiritual fathers can have in the church and throughout the world.

Pastor Tony's Story
Written by Pastor Tony Costa
Senior Pastor, Outside the Walls Ministries, Aurora, Colorado

I remember asking my son, "Why don't your friends come to church?" He honestly replied, "Dad, *church sucks*! It's not a place where my friends want to hang out." This rocked me and was a part of God's "hook" in getting me to attend the Building Brothers Leadership Training and understand more of the process that God wanted me to be on with the men in my church. I had to ask myself, "Where were the men and why weren't they attending my church?" God was opening my eyes to the great need in my church and the church at large in America.

The Building Brothers Leadership Training was one of the most impactful seminars I have ever attended. It put me in a safe environment where I could risk being completely transparent with my journey as a man and the larger journey within my church congregation. I walked away with some incredible tools to assist me in ministry.

The largest tool came into focus after the training—I started to see Building Brothers as a map. People need a "map" to assist them in finding their way or they just get lost and frustrated. I see Building Brothers as a great place to start, for church leadership to gather together and use this "map" to evaluate *where they are* and *where they need to go*. In self-evaluating, we found places where honestly, we stunk! And in others we were doing well. But the bottom line was that, as men, we needed a place to be "real" and help each other out in our daily battle.

It took a year of "percolating" after the training to begin the year-long process with our men. There were multiple roadblocks I had to deal with. The biggest was that I had to assist my leadership in understanding they weren't "doing what they were supposed to be doing" because they hadn't "become what God wanted them to become." Like most men, and most leaders, they had this backwards. As I met with each man in my leadership team I discovered that we didn't know where the "itch" was for our men. There are brothers who have gone before us, like Dan Schaffer, who have discovered where it is that men "itch." I realized that, as their pastor, if I wasn't going to do it, then who was?

We started the Building Brothers Phase I Training, and the men were a bit skeptical at first and asked some non-threatening questions. But the trust factor started to fall into place and this skepticism melted away. The men were going from just being "attenders" to becoming spiritually impacted and engaged in the process.

During that year, I was invited to try to build a spiritual bridge to the teenagers at a local youth detention facility. Many churches had tried and failed, giving up in a few months. Many of my men, some of whom used to be just "attenders," told me they *were* going to be a part of this. They said, "If you're going, I'm going." We now regularly have over thirty-five teens attending our interaction times, and I have witnessed fourteen of these youth accept Jesus into their lives. Also, I have seen my men planning how we can "love on them" as they leave the facility and reconnect into society.

My own children call me "Pops," and some of the men have picked up on this and are calling me by this same name. One man in our Building Brothers group recently asked, "Can I call you 'Pops'?" I told him, "Sure." Because of this relationship, he has told me that he didn't have a dad in his life. His father disappeared and doesn't seem to care if he lives or dies.

God has been correcting and directing us. I am very satisfied to see these young men being used in the transformational process in others' lives while I sit back and be their "dad." My actions tell them, you go "blow it out" in reaching the wounded, and I'll keep saying this message to them: (1) Jesus Christ came to seek and save the lost; (2) he came to destroy the work of the enemy; (3) he came to give his life for my behalf. Go tell the world these three facts, and I'll be here cheering for you on the sidelines so you can do this well. That's what this lost world is hungry for—a real man they can rely upon and call "Pops!"

Thoughts from a Woman's Heart
Written by Linda Tang
Proofreader for this book

No matter your age or how "together" you may be by the world's standards, *Spiritual Fathers: Restoring the Reproductive Church* will be a challenge to become the full man that God sees you becoming with time, work and dedication to achieve his goal. The path Dan Schaffer has outlined is truly for the committed and for those who can envision the bigger picture of how today transcends to tomorrow. The book is convicting and straightforward. The best part is that Dan provides a detailed roadmap in how to achieve the goal. It's easy to identify a problem and criticize without providing a solution, but Dan *has* the solutions in how to reach this goal. The effort men put in *now* will have lasting effects for future generations.

Not only did this book motivate me to pass it on to my husband and pastor, but stood as a resource of clear instruction and hope in how men can spiritually reach their fullest potential; and by doing so, they are giving their children every opportunity to develop and attain that realization as well.

The church has a great deal to look forward to by investing in their men and seeing to it that the future of the church and its children will continue to thrive collectively and individually—not just under the direction of a group of elders or a single pastor. Some of the work may be intense, but certainly necessary in order to obtain the goal (particularly, beginning with the earthly father/son relationship Dan discusses). In order to go forward with God in a healthy way, and to see him as a loving Father, the wounds or disappointments from the earthly father/son relationship must first be worked through. Though this can be painful, I felt that this was one of the most valuable points Dan made. He begins with the roots of that earthly, significant relationship, and says that you may need to *go back* in order to *move forward* with God. A healed foundation must be present so that the right relationship and perception of God can be formed or reestablished. This is an excellent, vital point for any man in a relationship with God, and I like how Dan says, "First things first."

I also found the statistics of parent participation and churchgoing children to be very informative—the man/father has a tremendous influence over his family and children, and his role as a leader is crucial. No offense taken at all as a woman; Men have a unique and strong presence that defines them as leaders, and together with their wives, helps them to establish and define the expectations, values and priorities of the household.

This book convicted me. The observations on present-day church conditions, backed up by statistics/facts, were insightful yet disheartening. And I enjoyed reading the touching stories about Dan's encounters with men, both here and abroad, regarding their spiritual transformations. *It only seems fair that the next book should be for the other side of the equation—Spiritual Mothers!*

Introduction

Lost in the Woods

My father, two brothers and I have always loved the outdoors. So in our family, one of the most important yearly events is going elk hunting together for several days.

One such time, we were on the Flattops in the Colorado Rockies near Trappers Lake. I love this beautiful area. My dad and my brother left at daybreak to hunt, but since I wasn't feeling well I started hiking to the area where we planned to hunt later in the day. I reached a meadow where I thought I might see some elk, and sat down to watch the area. The meadow was surrounded by black, downed timber.

I'd been sitting there for about two hours when a man who looked to be about thirty years old came rushing out of the timber. His eyes looked wild and his hair was disheveled. As he rushed into the clearing, he immediately noticed me sitting there and ran directly to me. He plopped down beside me and asked, "Where am I?"

Now notice, I was an eighteen-year-old kid looking at what I considered to be a grown man who, I assumed, should have known where he was. I didn't quite know how to answer him—we were in northwestern Colorado on the edge of the Flattops wilderness area. I finally looked at him and asked, "Well, where do you want to be?" He replied, "I don't know." So I asked, "Where did you start out from this morning?" He answered, "I don't know."

Think about his situation: He had left camp at six o'clock that morning. It was then two in the afternoon—eight hours later. He had been lost in black, dead, fallen timber and had no idea where he was that whole time.

In an attempt to get some sort of orientation I asked, "What did it look like where you were camped?" He began to describe a pond with lily pads. Fortunately for him, there was only one lily pad pond in probably fifteen or twenty square miles. So I knew he was only about two and a half miles from his camp.

In an effort to orient him, I looked to the north and pointed down to a county road about a mile away. I pointed to the left, which would be to the west, and I said, "That's the road that goes to Buford, and Buford is that way." He looked at me and replied, "No it isn't." Pointing to the right, he said, "Buford is *that* way." I said, "No, Buford is *this* way." He exclaimed, "No, Buford is *that* way!"

I don't know what you were like when you were eighteen years old, but my fuse was pretty short. I was getting a little irritated. Finally, I turned to the guy and got my nose about two inches away from his and asked, "Who's lost—me or you?" He answered, "I am." So I pointed to the west and announced, "Buford is *that* way."

The fellow continued to sit beside me for a considerable amount of time. While sitting there we saw a group of cow elk walk into a meadow stretching to the east. I told him that my brother had a cow license, and immediately he began to repeat, "Should I shoot it! Should I shoot it!" Even though he didn't have a license, would be breaking the law, and didn't know where in the world he was, he still wanted to shoot that elk!

Eventually he settled down, and after a while he asked me where the county road that went to the east would take him. I told him that it went to the top of Ripple Creek Pass; the area where his party had left the road to get into their camp. The man didn't have the personal confidence or skills to walk the trail the two-and-a-half miles to his camp. Instead, he walked the mile out to the road and caught a five-mile ride to the top of the pass. He then proceeded to walk eight miles to his camp. He couldn't bring himself to trust the trail that would have taken him "directly" to his camp.

The last I saw of the fellow was his red plaid coat and hatless head going down the trail to the county road. I am positive it was well after dark when he made it back to his camp.

I have written this book specifically focused and targeted to serve pastors and leaders within the church. As pastors and leaders you can probably identify with the lesson of this story. In your mind you may be saying, "I have had men who are lost around me most of my life. How do I help them find their way back to God?"

I invite you to journey through the rest of this book as we blaze a trail for men—a trail that will allow men to join with one another and rediscover their significance and identity through the pursuit of God and spiritual fatherhood.

Part I

A Church Lost in the Woods

Chapter 1

Are Men in Crisis?

Are the Church and its Men Lost in the Woods?

At the beginning of the 1990s—when God was beginning to do something significant in the lives of many men—we as men were in a similar situation to the lost man I just introduced. We knew things weren't right and we knew we needed direction, but we really didn't know where to go. It was almost as if God got our attention, looked us in the eye and said, "Who's lost—me or you?"

The Twentieth Century Church

In the last decades of the twentieth century the church was inundated with church growth strategies. However, during that same time the church's collective impact on its people and on the culture shrank continuously.

In his book, *The Bridger Generation*, Thom S. Rainer takes a look back over the past fifty years in the Christian community. He found that 65 percent of "Builders" (born between 1910 and 1946), 35 percent of "Boomers" (born between 1947 and 1964), and 15 percent of "Busters" (born between 1965 and 1976) made professions of faith. Only 4 percent of "Bridgers" (born between 1977 and 1994) are projected to make professions of faith.[1]

Following the Builders, or World War II generation, each generation has produced significantly less disciples than the preceeding generation. What has happened? *How did we go from a church that was impacting nearly two-thirds of the people in the culture to a church that now, after only four generations, is impacting only about 4 percent of the culture?* It is clear that the current strategies for church growth are not resulting in churches that are fulfilling the call and mission of the church.

3

What Is God's Primary Mission?

It is critically important to allow the New Testament to answer the following three questions:

What is God's primary mission and calling for the church?
What is God's primary mission and calling for a man?
What is God's primary mission and calling for a woman?

The clearest picture of the responsibilities and mission of the church are detailed in Ephesians 4:11–16. Verses 11–13 say, "It was he who gave some to be apostles, some to be prophets, some to be evangelists, and some to be pastors and teachers, to prepare God's people for works of service, so that the body of Christ may be built up until we all reach unity in the faith and in the knowledge of the Son of God and become mature." The primary role or mission of the church is to bring God's people—"the saints," as translated in many translations, to maturity and unity in order that they can do what God has called them to do.

If the mission of the church is to build up the saints to maturity and unity so that they can accomplish God's calling, then it is critically important to understand that call. In Genesis 1:28 we see God give the first command to mankind: "Be fruitful and multiply" (NASB)—meaning to reproduce biologically. In Matthew 28:19 we see Christ give the command to his people: "Go and make disciples"—meaning to reproduce spiritually. So it follows that the mission of God's people is to reproduce disciples who love the Lord their God with all of their heart and who love their neighbor as themselves (see Mark 12:28–31). The call for a man can be best summarized as becoming a spiritual father (1 John 2:12–14). And the call for a woman is to be a spiritual mother (Titus 2:3–5).

The answer to the three questions above can thus be stated: *The church has been given spiritually gifted individuals who build up God's people until they become spiritual fathers and mothers who reproduce generations of spiritual children who also grow into spiritual fathers and mothers.*

The Current Church

The current focus on seeker-friendly churches is not accomplishing this mission. We are attracting more and more immature Christians into

4

larger and larger adult nurseries where they expect others to give them milk and clean up their poop—and many of us spend countless hours obliging them. Babies are never able to reproduce! So is it any wonder that we don't see these nurseries reproducing, but rather just attracting more babies from other ineffective churches?

What will change this? First, the church must embrace the mission and calling that God laid out for it in Ephesians 4. Second, in order for the church to reproduce we must have spiritual fathers. The church currently has too few spiritual fathers able to mentor/disciple God's people into spiritual fatherhood and motherhood. It is essential that we begin to build the first generation of spiritual fathers. Third, the mature spiritual fathers must lay out a pathway to take men from immaturity to maturity so that the church is restored to being the reproductive body that God called it to be.

Spiritual Fatherhood

In 1 John 2:12–14, the Apostle John gives a significant description of three different levels of spiritual maturity. Throughout the letter, he consistently calls his readers "dear children." However, here he takes a noticeable departure from his, standard address, adding "fathers" and "young men" to his typical "dear children." When you look at the book as a whole, it seems at first glance that this passage doesn't fit where it is placed. Yet, this reference to "dear children," "fathers," and "young men" is found twice in verses 12–14. In the Hebrew culture and Greek language, repetition was used to show emphasis; the writer was saying, "This is very important, don't miss this." So we will take a closer look at this message to see what John had to say to his contemporaries as well as to us, the readers of today.

In verse 12, John starts by saying, "I write to you, dear children, because your sins have been forgiven on account of his name." He continues, "I write to you, fathers, because you have known him who is from the beginning." He ends the progression with, "I write to you, young men, because you have overcome the evil one." By using chronological age terminology, John distinguishes differences in levels of maturity among believers. Not only does John address the three categories again, but he also places the levels out of chronological order. Once again, the "fathers" are placed between the "dear children" and the "young men." Why would he do that? As we continue to look at the passage, I believe it will become clear that God has something special to communicate to us about the father role in particular.

We can summarize the definitions as they apply to spiritual maturity this way: "children" have come to a saving knowledge of Christ; "young men" are strong in the Word of God and have successfully fought the spiritual battle; and "fathers" know God intimately and have experienced a deep and fuller relationship with the "I AM"—the God of eternity (see Exodus 3:14–15). Now let's look at the reason that I believe the Spirit of God inspired John to communicate the levels out of their expected chronological order.

God is revealing here a key element of being a spiritual father. If we miss it, we miss the main point. This critical point is that you are not a spiritual father just because of your mature characteristics and deep relationship with the "I AM." *John placed the child and father together so that we would see the essential nature of reproduction in reaching and expressing maturity. You are a spiritual father because you have also been used to reproduce spiritual children.* Until a spiritually mature man reproduces and disciples Christlike maturity in others, he has no spiritual children and cannot be considered a spiritual father. A spiritual father reproduces spiritual children who have a passionate and intimate relationship with God the Father. The spiritual growth process of these children and young men must continue so that they also become spiritual fathers who reproduce spiritual children.

We must mature from children who have experienced salvation, to young men who know the Word of God and can wage the spiritual battle, to fathers who have walked intimately with God over a significant period of time and have been used to reproduce the next generation of spiritual fathers. If men are not reproducing spiritually, they have stopped short of experiencing and practicing full spiritual maturity.

Are We Presenting the Right Picture of Maturity?

In the church, we often replace the goal of having the characteristics of the "fathers" with the goal of having the characteristics of the "young men." That is, we present spiritual maturity as having the characteristics of the "young men," which calls our men to something short of what God is calling them to. We usually describe maturity as "knowing Scripture" and "being able to successfully wage spiritual battle." But mature men must also have a history of a deep and intimate relationship with the Living God and must be reproducing spiritual children. Those walking the pathway behind them can easily identify them as "spiritual fathers."

Has the church lost its understanding of spiritual reproduction? Can the church find itself while its men are still lost in the wilderness of confused identity and misplaced focus? Can we expect spiritually immature men to become spiritual fathers without a pathway being modeled by those who truly are spiritual fathers?

What Would a Pathway in Your Church Look Like?

This pathway is a continuum that starts with the foundational building blocks of the church. After considering the most essential elements that define a church, I believe they cannot be reduced to less than the following four key foundational areas. Below is my list of the four building blocks upon which the church is built:

1. *Worship.* Every body of believers must understand that worship is a key element of who they are, and that worship is not limited to services on Sunday morning. Rather, the church must present and teach worship as a lifestyle of obedience that brings glory to God.

2. *Truth.* Truth includes the Word of God, but also includes experience with the "Living Word"—Jesus Christ. Jesus told those who believed in him, "You will know the truth, and the truth shall set you free ... So if the Son sets you free, you will be free indeed" (John 8:32, 36). Not only do we need the written Word, but we also need to develop an intimate relationship with the Living Word. Any church that doesn't focus on the truth, Jesus Christ, will not be an effective church for very long.

3. *Reproduction.* In most churches, if the leaders talk about "reproduction" what they are really talking about is evangelism. Is evangelism all there is to reproduction? No. You can evangelize and fill the church with spiritual babies; reproduction doesn't happen until the babies mature and are themselves reproducing. For example, your family name will die unless your sons reproduce. Reproduction is the legacy of a healthy family, and reproduction in the church produces a healthy, ongoing church.

4. *Building male leadership.* Here we come to a critical question the church must answer: Is building men into mature, godly leaders foundational to the church? Yes! Is this biblical? Yes—Jesus and the apostles, as well as the church fathers, demonstrated this principle in their models for founding the church. So why do we have such a difficult time agreeing on this as a church?

The Church Leadership Core

If we can agree that the building of men is foundational to the health and continuance of the church, then the next step in the pathway is building a church leadership core that is pursuing God, modeling this passion for God, and able to reproduce it in others. It's been said that *we teach what we know, but we reproduce what we are.* I can challenge you to be spiritually mature and a man of passion for God, but if someone has not reproduced in you, it is impossible for you to be used to reproduce this in others. Are we willing to let God so impact and "impregnate" us with his Word and his Spirit that we will be compelled to become spiritual fathers? This is the piece that's missing in most churches—**and it must start with the leadership of the church.**

We have too few spiritual fathers in the church. My desire is to serve the church by assisting in bringing a leadership core group together and helping them to reproduce the Father's heart in others.

Four Universal Barriers

In order for leaders to be reproductive for Christ they must first understand and overcome the barriers that keep men from pursuing God. There are many things that keep men from pursuing God, but I have identified four barriers that seem to universally affect men.

1. *All men experience a father vacuum.* This vacuum is caused by their relationship with their earthly father. Each of us has experienced imperfect fathering and this fathering produces the vacuum and shapes our view of the heavenly Father. This barrier is rarely addressed in the normal life of the church. Until men address this distortion of their view of God they will be inhibited in their efforts to freely and fully pursue God.

2. *The church lacks a safe masculine environment.* Without a safe place, a man will not find his identity in the church and he will not expose those issues within him that God must change. We need a place in the church where a man can come home to, live in and experience transformation.

3. *Men do not trust their leaders and their leaders do not trust them.* The model of leadership within the church causes this lack of trust. In order to follow someone into the pursuit of God, we must trust him. Men who are biblical servant leaders build unity and trust. We must become men who can be trusted so that other men will join us in the pursuit of God.

4. *Men see their relationship with God as an obligation rather than an opportunity.* There are two practices we must stop: (1) trying to earn the right to approach God which leads us to isolation; (2) trying to follow a formula that we feel will obligate God to give us a life free of pain, which ultimately leads to bitterness. Isolation and bitterness will prevent us from grasping the opportunity to be in relationship with God. It is only when we move past these barriers that we can fully pursue a passionate relationship with our Father God.

Without a pathway and models to serve as guides for the journey, how will these barriers be broken down? Without a core group of men willing to allow God to reproduce in them what they want to reproduce in others, it will be almost impossible for a man to go from where he is to where he needs to be in Christ.

The Essential Nature of a Pathway

If we have been able to help men fill their father vacuum with a proper view of their Father God, then we must create a safe place within the church experience where a man can feel he is spiritually at home. We must learn to become servant leaders whom others will trust to follow into the process of pursuing God. It is only as we learn to trust one another that we will be able to join in the pursuit of God. And finally, we must grasp the opportunity to be in relationship with God. Therefore, it is critical that we intentionally focus on removing the barriers that are keeping men from pursuing God.

Why does this process not just happen automatically? Most churches will readily admit that they don't have a pathway to take men from spiritual immaturity (childhood) to spiritual maturity (spiritual fatherhood). I find that we don't really believe that the building of men is foundational to the church and therefore are unwilling to expend the energy and resources to make it happen. We are part of a consumer/program culture that sends people to programs to get their needs met rather than joining with them in a life process. At a very basic level we are trying to get a reproductive result from a production or program method. You rarely, if ever, obtain reproduction from programmatic methods. In order to change this, we as leaders must become the first-fruits of the process, and then, through "who we are," reach out to change the culture of the church. Only then can we hope to restore a reproductive environment in the church—one that will reproduce spiritual fathers who are reproducing.

A Pioneer Mentality

For many churches, the missing piece is that they do not have core leaders pioneering the process and blazing the pathway to take men from immaturity to maturity. We as leaders must first become what we want the men of the church to become. This pathway needs to be visible, definable, joinable, and normative. It becomes the normal, expected process when the functional leaders of the church are committed to, and walking alongside, their men on this pathway.

I want to challenge you to read on. Journey with me as we focus on the church and detail a pathway that will lead men out of the wilderness and into the reproductive church that God designed it to be.

---

1 Thom S. Rainer, *The Bridger Generation* (Nashville: Broadman & Holman Publishers, 1997), 16.

SPIRITUAL FATHERS

Chapter 2

Are the Church and Culture in Crisis?

It was obvious that the longer the man in our story was lost, the more frantic and fearful he became. In the last decade of the twentieth century, many men experienced similar feelings, and their actions clearly expressed a desire to find a way out of the wilderness.

An Explosion of Men

By the beginning of the 1990s, a steady decline in the involvement of men in the church had reached a crisis point: church pews were filled with women and children but few men. It seems this trend was reflected in the problems of divorce, crime and teen pregnancy. In the midst of this, God gave birth to Promise Keepers. With approximately 4,200 men in attendance at the first conference in 1991, we saw his Spirit beginning to stir men's hearts. In 1992 the number grew to 22,000, and in 1993 there were 56,000 men. Attendance then exploded to 250,000 in 1994 and 750,000 in 1995 and culminated in 1996 with 1.2 million men attending conferences across the country.

Men Abandoning the Church

During this time many men's lives were deeply changed as they hungered to know God and discover his pathway to godliness. But this awakened hunger was not always fed when they returned home to their churches, and their lives eventually produced little lasting change in the church and the culture. While attendance at Promise Keepers events was growing exponentially, we believed that men were returning to the church in comparative numbers. However, the opposite was actually taking place. A George Barna survey in 1992 found that 42 percent of men in America attended church. By 1996 that number had dropped to 28 percent, *which shows that nearly one-third of the men in church in 1992 had left by 1996.*

Even though 1996 saw the height of the impact of Promise Keepers, it became clear that the revival we had hoped for was not happening. The movement of Promise Keepers had only slowed the hemorrhage of men exiting the church. Why were these men leaving, and what could we do to change the situation?

Crisis in the Church

Many people in larger churches feel that Christianity is growing because their church is experiencing rising attendance, finances are healthy and new building programs can accommodate their growth. Yet, almost every quantitative measure paints a different picture. With this in mind, go back to Thom S. Rainer's numbers from the last chapter. He found that 65 percent of Builders, 35 percent of Boomers, and 15 percent of Busters made professions of faith—while it is estimated that less than 4 percent of Bridgers will make professions of faith. Reflecting on these figures, what would you say about a company that went from a 65 percent market share to less than 4 percent? The business would be in danger of going bankrupt, and you'd be selling your stock!

This issue became clear to me when I heard Josh McDowell speak to the National Coalition of Men's Ministries. Regarding the youth of the church, he stated that indications predict less than 6 percent of the children who grow up in the church remain there as adults. Put that together with less than 4 percent of the population making a profession of faith in Christ, and the crisis of the church can easily be seen. *The only conclusion to be drawn is that we have failed.* This failure is heightened by the fact that the majority of Christian men today have not personally embraced the Great Commission within their own families. We are not building up spiritual fathers who are reproducing into the generations to come. This trend accounts for the slow death of the church that we are witnessing today.

Fathers and Faith Communities

In 1994 officials in the Swiss government, recognizing the value of faith communities and their impact on the culture as a whole, decided to send out a special survey along with their census. They looked at churches, synagogues, mosques, and any other worship center they could identify as a "faith community." And because they saw value in them, they wanted to identify the primary factor that determined whether children grew up and remained in that faith community as adults. This is a summary of some of the data from that research.[1]

IMPACT OF PARENTS' PARTICIPATION IN FAITH COMMUNITIES ON CHILDREN

		MOTHER		
		REGULAR PARTICIPANT	**IRREGULAR PARTICIPANT**	**NON-PARTICIPANT**
FATHER	**REGULAR PARTICIPANT**	Reg. **33%**	**38%**	**44%**
		Irreg. **41%**	**37%**	**31%**
		Non **26%**	**25%**	**25%**
	IRREGULAR PARTICIPANT	Reg. **3%**		
		Irreg. **59%**		
		Non **38%**	**CHILDREN**	
	NON-PARTICIPANT	Reg. **2%**		
		Irreg. **37%**		
		Non **61%**		

First, take a look at the father's quadrant, where the father is a regular, irregular or non-participant in a faith community. Second, look at the mother's quadrant, where she is a regular, irregular or non-participant. If both the mother and father are regular participants, 33 percent of their children participate in the faith community. If the father is regular and the mother is irregular, 38 percent of the children participate regularly. If the mother is a non-participant, the children's involvement goes up to 44 percent. As the mother's participation decreases, the children's participation increases. What is going on here? I believe this phenomenon indicates that a father's spiritual commitment has the greatest influence on the value his children place on spiritual matters.

Let's compare this with the mother being the regular participant. When the father is the irregular participant, only 3 percent of the children are participants—as compared to 38 percent when the situation is reversed. *The father's commitment has 12 times the impact of the mother's commitment.* When the father is a non-participant, the children's involvement drops to 2 percent—as opposed to 44 percent when the situation is reversed. *When compared to the mother being the non-participant, this demonstrates 22 times the impact!*

Whether we like it or not, a man's involvement or lack of it in spiritual matters will, to a great extent, determine his children's openness to God. Not only do we as men have the opportunity to impact our children, but also to fatherless children who God places in our lives. Do you realize that God has given you an incredible amount of power—almost the power of spiritual life and death? Could it be that the crisis within the church is a crisis of men not becoming spiritual fathers?

Crisis in the Culture

I can clearly see the power a father has and how his physical and spiritual absence has created a crisis in our culture. Almost every current challenge facing our culture, families, and churches can be traced to or related to the absence of men and their ineffectiveness in fulfilling their responsibilities. I could write volumes and share pages of statistics on this issue, but I would rather challenge you to look into your own experience and see if this is true. A pastor recently told me, "I don't need to be convinced by the statistics; I just have to look at my congregation to see that fathers are not reproducing."

Crisis of the Masculine Lie

In the 1950s, men were portrayed by the media, in television shows like *Father Knows Best* and *Bonanza*, as wise protectors. Men were represented as strong, valuable contributors to the family and the culture. Moving from that time to the present, a radical change has occurred in the way the media and culture represent men and their roles. In contrast, the current image depicts men as imbeciles at best—easily manipulated by their appetites and desires—and, at worst, as the very evil that is destroying our people and culture. When men are shown in a positive role, that role is feminized or overtly effeminate; it is hard for many of us to identify positive male characteristics.

We are repeatedly bombarded by the media with this lie, and the cumulative toll is extremely high in men's lives and within the culture. How do you feel the pressure of this lie?

The Opportunity to Leave a Legacy

When I look at men in the culture and within the church, I see men who are insecure, hesitant and uninvolved. They seem to be waiting for the women in their lives to affirm and define their value; yet they are clearly hungry to be significant and to leave a legacy that matters!

Virtually all of the current research shows the terrible cost of absent fathers to the church, the family and the culture. But what God created us to do, he enables us to do. It is essential that we call men back to the image and identity that the Creator laid out for us.

When Christ set out to build his church, didn't he invest himself personally in the training, encouragement, and building up of a small group of men? Shouldn't we follow his model by working to produce servant leaders—spiritual fathers who will pass on a legacy of growth, Christlikeness, and spiritual maturity to future servant leaders?

God offers us the opportunity to mature spiritually and join him in the work of spiritual reproduction. Do you hunger for this? We must begin the work of building men who will become servant leaders and spiritual fathers to the next generation.

The Next Step

In order to leave a legacy we must be men who passionately pursue a relationship with God. Many of us are kept from that pursuit due to the relationship that we experienced with our earthly father. Our relationship with our earthly father can distort the relationship we could have with our heavenly Father. It is time to expose our father vacuum to our Father God so that he can heal it.

1 Robbie Low, "The Truth About Men & Church," *Touchstone*, June 2003, Volume 16, Issue 5, http://touchstonemag.com/archives/article.php?id=16-05-024-v.

Part II

*Building a Safe
Place for Men*

Chapter 3

The Father Vacuum

In our opening story the lost man was afraid to take the trail that would have led him back to his camp in about an hour. He wasn't able to trust himself or me. It could have been that he hadn't been taught the skills nor the confidence needed to pioneer a trail. To step out into the unknown, we need the skill, the confidence, and the compass that will keep us from getting lost in the woods. For many of us, the insecurity caused by the "father vacuum" keeps us on the old destructive trails.

What Is the Father Vacuum?

The father vacuum is the result of wounds left by our fathers. When we are threatened or hurt, we question our value and competence. This vacuum—a space devoid of anything—is always trying to fill itself with something. Many of us try to fill it with things that stroke our egos and make us feel worthy and valuable. The void makes us susceptible to addictive behaviors; thus, we are drawn to alcohol, drugs, sex, work, power, money, etc.

I believe each one of us has a father vacuum to a degree. Some have fathers who have tried to model God's love, and therefore the vacuum is small. For others, whose fathers were absent, distant, or abusive, the vacuum is larger. Whatever the size, this vacuum must be filled by our Father God. When we allow him to appropriately fill this void, we can begin to experience self-worth, healing, and freedom. If we do not, the issues with our earthly fathers will continue to block us from enjoying a full and intimate relationship with our heavenly Father, as well as with the people we love.

The Heart of the Message*

Note to readers: from this chapter on, each chapter contains an introductory overview called, "The Heart of the Message."

The father vacuum can only be filled by the affirmation of value or blessing from the "fathers" in our life. Earthly fathers can see the opportunity they have to extend this blessing and release their children, but this will only fill a portion of the vacuum. Other men can affirm and bless us, and that will bring a measure of healing as well; but it is only as we use these temporal blessings to allow us to accept the blessing of our Father God that we are free to fully pursue God and become spiritual fathers. This gift of a blessing from God our Father coming to us through a godly man is what I mean by "the father's blessing."

At a Building Brothers training, I extended an invitation for men who had never experienced their earthly father's affirmation and blessing to step forward and experience another man speaking God the Father's blessing to them. The first man down the aisle was the pastor of the host church who had been a pastor for over thirty years. Although he desired to give this kind of blessing to his congregation, he was struggling with never having received his earthly father's blessing; therefore, was unable to accept his Father God's blessing and participate in blessing others. Behind him came a man in his thirties. Next, was a prominent dentist, tears running off his chin.

Everywhere around the world my travels have taken me, I have seen the intensity of this need for the father's blessing. It's been unmistakable that men *and* women—who also struggle with the father vacuum—long for a positive father figure in their lives who loves them and affirms their value.

If fathers have such power over our emotional well-being, what impact do they have on our spiritual well-being? As I have listened to men's stories, it has become clear that our view of God is largely determined by our relationship with our earthly father. If Dad was distant, we expect God to be distant. If Dad was judgmental, we expect God to be judgmental. If Dad left us, we fear that God will leave us. Many of us have remained distant from God, our heavenly Father, because we have never had deep issues resolved with our earthly father.

So how can we help men and women find healing in order to move forward into a close, loving, intimate relationship with their heavenly Father? Doesn't it need to start with us?

Going Deeper*

Note to readers: From this chapter on, the "Going Deeper" section of each chapter follows the introductory overview called "The Heart of the Message" and further develops that overview.

How Important is it to Address the Father Vacuum?

A pastor friend recounted an experience in seminary in which the professor asked the students to take an inventory that analyzed their relationship with their father. Without giving any explanation, about one month later, the professor gave them the same inventory again, but asked them to answer it according to the way they related to God. He then brought the two inventories and their responses together. What do you think it showed? As the students compared the two inventories, they saw little difference in how they described their relationship with their father and their relationship with God.

Your pattern of seeing God is influenced by the relationship you experienced with your father. Some of you have had a difficult relationship with your father that has made it difficult for you to experience God as a positive heavenly Father. Some of you have had the father vacuum exposed and have begun to have a healthy view of God. Others will find themselves in the middle. Many of us have experienced God's goodness at some level but haven't fully experienced him as Father because we are still impacted negatively by our relationship with our earthly father.

Adolescent Elephant Gangs

A number of years ago, I watched on PBS a *National Geographic* program filmed in South Africa.[i] Game wardens in Pilanesberg National Park began finding rhinos that had been viciously attacked. They looked like they were on their last leg: they had scars on their sides and many of them had puncture wounds throughout their hardened bodies. The game wardens didn't know what was attacking them, or why, but they were afraid of losing their entire rhino population.

After studying the bizarre situation, do you know what they found? The attackers were groups of adolescent male elephants. To try to discover what was causing the violent behavior, the game wardens captured a few of these elephants and tested them for substances that might be altering their behavior. But the only abnormality they could find was elevated levels of testosterone for their age.

It was then that the wardens realized what had happened. Two years before, they had decided they needed to reduce the elephant population, so they removed the most mature bulls from the herd. Left unchecked by older bulls, the young bulls matured too quickly. They then gathered into adolescent gangs and began to prey upon the rhinos within their territory.

Understanding the situation, the game wardens resolved to introduce mature bulls back into the population. After doing so, they recaptured the young adolescents and tested them again. Their testosterone levels had dropped. And the adolescent bulls were no longer in gangs and were no longer attacking rhinos.

We can step into dangerous territory when we relate human behavior to animal behavior, but we're talking about a dynamic that I believe does have application. *When you remove the father from the culture and the family, you remove both the restraint and the model of mature male behavior; this is destructive for the children and the culture.* There is no denying the fact that this destructive circle is playing out in our culture!

Robbie Low, a vicar in England, put it well when he said, "No father—no family—no faith. Winning and keeping men is essential to the community of faith and vital to the work of all mothers and the future salvation of our children."[ii] When one reviews published research it is clear that the source of most our problems in our culture can be directly linked to the relationship (or lack thereof) between fathers and their children. Do you see the cost to society and the individual? This impacts every area of our culture and each one of us.

If we lose the fathers, we will lose the next generation. When I read Exodus 20:4–6, I'm greatly encouraged. This passage states that the children of those fathers who don't worship God are judged to the fourth generation, but the children of the fathers who obediently worship God are blessed to the thousandth generation. The negative impact of a father is significant, but the positive impact of a father is immeasurable.

The Horse Whisperer

Let's look at a couple of sections from the book, *The Man Who Listens to Horses*. Hollywood produced a movie with a similar title, but that's not what I'm referring to. Monty Roberts, the author of the book, is renown as a horse whisperer who "breaks" horses gently. He has demonstrated his amazing techniques to heads of state, presidents, and kings and queens. Let me take you on a quick journey through his life and what he eventually experienced as a man in his 50s.

Monty's father was a horse breaker by trade. He broke horses in a very violent fashion. He would run the horses to exhaustion and then load them with weights to where the horses would actually break down and collapse. His final act would be to physically tie them down and stand on them to gain dominance.

When Monty was seven, his dad decided it was probably time for him to try his hand at breaking horses. He told his son he could have two horses to break and warned him, "A horse is a dangerous machine, and you'd be wise to remember that. You hurt them first—or they'll hurt you." Even as a young child, Monty didn't feel comfortable with the process of violently breaking horses. He asked his father if he could have some extra time with the two horses. Monty took them to a back pasture and began working with them. On the third day, he had a saddle on one of the horses!

Monty had this to say about that day:

> Wildly excited by what I had accomplished, I ran
> immediately to the house to tell my father. I asked him to
> come and watch … When we arrived he said nothing …
> Then moving quietly and calmly, I reached up as high as I
> could and slid a saddle on [the horse's] back. It was for
> me a magical experience. At this point, I looked up at my

father, who was staring at me with his mouth open. I was uncertain how to read that look, but I was hoping it was astonishment and maybe pride at my accomplishing this after only three days. Slowly he stood up, still fixing me with his look that could have meant any number of things. "What the hell am I raising?" were the first words he uttered.[iii]

Monty's father grabbed a four-foot stall chain and beat his seven-year-old son so severely that he had to be rushed to the emergency room. I can picture Monty now. He had done something in three days that took his father six weeks to accomplish. He wanted to run to his daddy and seek his approval for what he'd been able to do. But his father wasn't able to move beyond the phrase, "You hurt them first—or they'll hurt you."

The physical beatings continued until Monty was fifteen, and the scars this left behind drove a wedge between father and son. When Monty was fifty-five years old, his dying mother made one last request for these two estranged men to come together. Read Monty's heartbreaking words:

> On the day my father sat down, finally, to watch me start a raw horse, he was well into his seventies. I was no longer desperate for his approval, though I was still a son who would have welcomed his father's belated blessing. I was also a man in his fifties who had by this time started more than 6,500 horses. Apart from all the working horses, I had trained Thoroughbreds who had gone on to win major stakes races all over the world ... I had spent my life going against my father, and now finally, because my mother had made it her dying wish, he would see where it had taken me.[iv]

Monty got the first horse and brought it into the ring. He ended up riding the horse after working with it for only twenty minutes. As Monty repeated this feat with horse after horse, his father continued to watch him but took every chance he was given to verbally put down or deny his son's amazing work with these animals.

At the end of many hours, Monty responded to his father. This is how he describes the interaction:

> By end of that day my father had seen me start more horses than he could have broken in six weeks. He came down from the viewing deck and we stood outside, hardly able to see each other's face in the dusk. "What do you think of that?" ... "Keep doing it that way," I heard him say, "and they'll get you."
>
> Up at the house that night, my mother seemed especially anxious to know what he thought ... She skirted the topic for a while, then finally she asked, "So, Marvin, how'd you enjoy what you saw today?" "Fine."
>
> My mother pressed. "What do you think of it all?" My father replied, "It's suicide." There would be no end in her lifetime (or his, for that matter) to the rift.[V]

Monty's piercing last statement concerning this interaction with his father was, "But the horse remained a towering symbol of the space between father and son."[VI]

Monty Roberts desired to connect with and be affirmed by his father. But his father's inability to respond impacted the family tremendously and will continue to do so.

The importance of a father's affirmation should never be underestimated!

My Story

Let me share my own story.

My mom and dad both became believers as young adults. This fact would determine much of their impact on me in years to come. My dad came from a really tough background. When he was in his early twenties, he served in the Coast Guard during the Second World War. He began to have chest pain and thought he was having a heart attack, so he went to the infirmary. They tested him, but his heart was not the problem.

What they found instead was scar tissue all throughout his chest. As a small child at the age of seven or eight, he had been forced to lift such heavy sacks of grain (about 100 pounds each), that the muscles inside his chest actually tore and caused scar tissue to form. He worked hard most of his young life and didn't have much pain. But when he got into the Coast Guard he wasn't working as hard physically to keep those lesions broken, and the scar tissue began to tie up his chest.

When my father was seventeen years old and still at home, his appendix burst. His stepfather wouldn't pay for the surgery; so Dad worked bent over—in danger of dying—until he made enough money, along with his mother's egg money, to have the operation.

That's just a small glimpse of what my dad went through. Does that sound like a pretty severe background to you? But like most young men, I really didn't understand my dad. When I was in my late teens, I was pretty angry and didn't understand what was causing this anger. After this had affected me for a significant part of my life, I was about to discover the underlying cause and experience freedom in this area.

Through the years, hunting became the primary way for us to spend time together while connecting with one another. One time, when I was about thirty years old, we went elk hunting and decided to rent two horses. They turned out to be awful horses! One had two bald spots on its face from the buckles on its halter. The other had a sore on its withers, and every time you would get on it you'd have a little rodeo for a while!

There we were—outfitted like the Pillsbury Doughboy because of the cold, and struggling to keep these obstinate horses under control and on the trail. Dealing with the horses finally triggered my dad to start talking about his childhood and how the animals on the farm had really made his life worthwhile. He talked about how he had farmed with them and took care of them and how those animals were one of the bright spots in his young life.

In the midst of that, he began to tell me about a time when he was five years old and was in the back of the old farmhouse whittling wood in the wood box. He slipped and cut himself, and said a filthy German phrase. He didn't know what it meant but he had heard his stepfather say it. At that moment, his stepfather came in and began to beat him to the extent that his mother actually had to intervene. What he told me next on that hillside changed me. He said, "You know, I can still feel the imprint of his hand on my face."

Dad was sixty-five years old then. For the first time in my life, instead of seeing my dad as a father, an icon, I saw him as that wounded little boy. You know what God did in that instant? He began to show me that in most cases, when somebody has been abused like my dad was, the next generation of abuse is worse than the first. If the father is abusive, the abused son becomes even more abusive. In my case, because God intervened, that did not happen. God broke the cycle of abuse when my parents committed themselves to him as young adults. I realize I had become angry because of what my father had not been able to give me. I now understand that he had given me much more than I had any right to expect. The moment I understood that, God began to heal me. He allowed me to see my father in a different way and to understand my Father God's care for me.

I never told my dad what I was angry about. Do you know why? Because there was no longer any reason to. I left that mountain being thankful instead of embittered.

Have you resolved the issues between you and your father, or are you still harboring anger or unforgiveness? Your father may have been like mine—basically good—but you are left with some holes that need to be filled. Or your father may have been abusive and/or physically or emotionally absent. In any case, your relationship with God and your capacity to be used by him in ministry will be largely determined by the depth and intensity of the father vacuum. You can't give away what you don't have. How can we help others fill their father vacuum if we haven't allowed God to fill ours?

Filling the Father Vacuum

When Jesus was baptized by John and came up out of the water, the Holy Spirit descended on him like a dove. "And a voice from heaven said, 'This is my Son, whom I love, with him I am well pleased'" (Matthew 3:16–17). Let me ask you a few questions about this passage. At what time was this in Christ's ministry? Wasn't it at the very beginning? Had he done anything to deserve this blessing and affirmation?

Not in an earthly sense. He hadn't healed anyone and he hadn't performed any miracles. I want you to see that God was affirming Christ because of who he was, not because of what he had done.

We tend to feel that we can win our dad's approval if we just do the right things. Have you tried to live the Christian life, trying to do the right things so that you could hear Gods words of approval to you? If this is the model, if this is what God did for his own Son—to release him for his ministry—how important is it for us to come to a point of accepting God the Father's blessing? Does this blessing apply to you? I know it does!

In Romans 8:16–17 Paul writes, "The Spirit himself testifies with our spirit that we are God's children. Now if we are children, then we are heirs—heirs of God and co-heirs with Christ ..." This passage establishes the value to us of the Father God's blessing of Christ. Everything that was Christ's is yours and mine. Why? By virtue of our adoption into God's family. So let me ask again, does the blessing apply to you?

Have you ever experienced your earthly father's blessing? Most of us never have. When I turned forty-eight years old, I received a very special birthday card from my mom and dad. I don't know what prompted them, other than the Spirit of God, but they both sat down and wrote things about me. They wrote what they were feeling when I was in my mother's womb and how they promised me to God—things I had never known about. They didn't write paragraphs, just three or four sentences. But they affirmed that God had already chosen me as his son. This helped to reaffirm and release God's destiny in my life. I read the birthday card with tears running down my face. Why? I felt that I had already received my father's blessing, but I experienced the power of the continuing affirmation and blessing. There is no minimum or maximum age limit on the intrinsic, deep need for our dad's approval.

The Father's Blessing

Let's go back to Matthew 3:17. I want to challenge you to make this blessing personal by changing the pronouns and speaking this verse out loud: *I am Your son, whom You love, with __me__ You are well pleased.* Repeat it again! *I am Your son, whom You love, with __me__ You are well pleased.* Are you able to accept this statement? Will you live in response to it? Psalm 149:4 says, "The LORD takes delight in his people." Do you struggle with the truth that God delights in you and is pleased with you as his son?

It's really difficult for me to visualize God's delight and pleasure with me. Can you visualize God sitting on his heavenly throne looking down on you and saying, "Look at my son! See him? I'm delighted in him!"? Do you have children? If so, know that God delights in you like you did when your kids were little—when you walked in the front door and saw your child and responded by beaming with pleasure just because it was your child. Is it hard for you to visualize that God is responding that way to you right now?

Isaac and Jacob

In Genesis 27, God gives us a pattern for blessing another person. In this story, Isaac attempts to bless Esau, his oldest son. Isaac sends Esau out to hunt some game for him to eat. Rebekah helps deceive Isaac so that Jacob, their youngest son, receives the blessing. She dressed Jacob to smell and feel like Esau and sent him in to Isaac who was blind. Isaac said to Jacob, "You smell like Esau but you sound like Jacob." In addition, his mother had put goatskins on Jacob's arms so he would feel hairy like his brother.

How close do you have to be to someone to know their unique smell and feel? You almost have to have your nose on their skin. It is clear that during this blessing Isaac was in close physical contact with the person he was blessing. A blessing is much more significant with meaningful touch.

Gary Smalley and John Trent, in their groundbreaking book, *The Blessing,* identify five elements of a blessing as illustrated in this passage:[vii] (1) Isaac exhibited meaningful touch that was close and intimate. (2) He spoke the blessing out loud. Isaac didn't know he was speaking to Jacob; he thought he was giving his blessing to Esau. But his verbal blessing still stood. (3) Isaac communicated high value by confirming God's abundant provision for his son. (4) Isaac verbally pictured a special future by describing Jacob's unique position in his family and culture. (5) Isaac demonstrated his commitment to Jacob's future by refusing to reverse the blessing even after it was revealed that Jacob had stolen the blessing from Esau.

These are the same elements that the men and women in our churches are hungry for today. They're desperate to experience meaningful affirmation from the Father God; and they need to experience it through us, and from us, as well.

---

1. **Meaningful Touch** – make physical contact with the individual who is being blessed (Genesis 27:26).
2. **Spoken Word** – blessing needs to be spoken out loud to the person being blessed (Genesis 27:27-29).
3. Attaching "high value" to the one being blessed (Genesis 27:28-29).
4. Picturing a "special feature" for the one being blessed (Genesis 27:28-29).
5. An "active commitment" to fulfill the blessing (Genesis 27: 30-33).

German Tears

A couple of years ago, I was in northern Germany and shared this same message in a town just outside of Frankfort. There were about 900 men at the conference, which is a very large attendance for a conference in Germany. I began to share this message about the father vacuum. It was somewhat awkward working with a translator: you don't have the same rhythm, and things aren't always said the same way. The translator even has the opportunity to misinterpret or manipulate what you're trying to communicate. At the end of the message, I planned to give the men an opportunity to respond to what they had heard. My desire, and what God had laid on my heart, was that I wanted the men who had experienced the blessing of their earthly father to gather around and speak God's blessing to those who hadn't yet received the blessing.

I asked the men who had not experienced the blessing of their earthly father to stand up. I expected that only about 10 percent would respond because Germans tend to be reserved. I believed there would be plenty of men left who could pray for them and give them the blessing. Do you know what happened? I was shocked to see 90 percent of the men stand up! They had tears running off their noses and chins. Eight hundred and ten men were standing and less than one hundred men remained who could pray for them. I ended up praying for all the men myself, verbalizing God's blessing to them as they placed their hands on each other's shoulders. That's all I could do.

Months later returned to northern Germany, and I was again asked to speak about the father vacuum at a gathering of men. I saw the same response again—men standing with tears streaming down their faces. When I was asked later on to speak to mixed audiences of both men and women, the response was the same for the women as it was for the men. Young women and older women stood and wept. It became apparent to me that women can participate and support one another in the healing process, but only a man who has had his father vacuum filled by God can approach women as a father and affirm the blessing. Healed men are essential in meeting this foundational need within the church and the culture.

Extending the Father's Blessing to Others

Do you see the importance? We must reach a point where we accept the blessing from God and then allow him to use us to extend "the father's blessing" to others. If we as men don't receive healing for our father vacuum and then extend the blessing to others, we're going to see succeeding generations of damaged people around us looking for affirmation in artificial and unsatisfying ways. Many who are caught up in drug or alcohol abuse, sexual addiction, and all sorts of other addictive behaviors are trying to prove, by the way they stroke themselves, that they're worthy. I'm not claiming that fatherlessness causes all those damaging behaviors, but I am saying it predisposes men to be susceptible to them. Fatherlessness predisposes men to pornography. It predisposes men to misuse of alcohol and drugs, to workaholism, and to materialism. It predisposes our daughters to damaging sexual activity. The absence of a blessing tends to prejudice women towards addictive relationships and men towards addictive behaviors. The gift of the blessing delivers freedom.

It can be difficult for men who have had good fathers to understand the huge hole that other men are experiencing. They look at those other men and say, "What's wrong with them?" Without realizing their own father vacuum, they don't understand the importance and magnitude of the father vacuum most men experience. My informal observations indicate that between 70 and 90 percent of the men and women in the church are struggling at some level with a father vacuum. Some suffer very significantly, others not so much—but it's still crippling them from being all God wants them to be.

Do you see the importance of passing this blessing along? Do you see how foundational this is for us to become healed men so that God can use us to pass his healing on to so many others who desperately need it?

As you experience healing, God will bring you opportunities to exercise the power of the blessing in the lives of others. Will you grasp those opportunities?

The blessing begins the healing process, but that healing process must be fostered in a safe place for men. What does that safe place look like?

---

[i] *Reflections on Elephants*, produced by Dereck and Beverly Joubert (Wildlife Films Botswana for the National Geographic Society, Washington, DC, 1994).

[ii] Robbie Low, "The Truth About Men & Church," *Touchstone*, June 2003, Volume 16, Issue 5, http://touchstonemag.com/archives/article.php?id=16-05-024-v.

[iii] Monty Roberts, *The Man Who Listens to Horses* (New York: Random House, 1996), 55–56.

[iv] Ibid., 200–201.

[v] Ibid., 207–8.

[vi] Ibid., 208.

[vii] Gary Smalley and John Trent, *The Blessing* (New York: Pocket Books, 1986), 27.

Chapter 4

How Do We Create a Safe Place for Men?

Someone who is lost needs a safe place to find where he's at and to gain the skills that will prevent him from getting further lost as he finds his way home. Even if a man is motivated in this area, where does he go to find help and who does he trust to help him? You have to experience a safe place to offer a safe place. Just like I had to ask the man lost in the woods, "Who's lost—me or you?" we need to ask that of each other in the church.

The Heart of the Message

Effective ministry to men is the process of developing relationships that become a platform for change. This requires a *safe masculine environment* that encourages trust, open-ended questions, application of God's truth and prayer.

At a training seminar, I asked the men present, "Is the church a masculine or a feminine place?" They immediately answered, "It is a feminine place." When asked further how that affected them, they shared that it made them hesitant, timid, and restrained.

The majority of the pastors I interact with have never heard this message from the men in their churches. In contrast, what they usually hear is a vocal group of women asking why the church is such a male-dominated institution. Yet, while men have not voiced their discomfort, haven't they spoken loudly with their lack of involvement?

As I noted at the beginning of chapter 2, at the height of the Christian men's movement in the 1990s, when we felt that we were seeing a spiritual awakening, men were actually leaving the church in unprecedented numbers. Conscientious, positive, purposeful men were finding more value and purpose outside the church than in it. How, then, can we call men back to the church to find purpose in their relationship with God?

In the last chapter we saw how the father vacuum can create a major barrier to a man's passionate pursuit of God. Could the lack of a safe masculine environment within the church be an equally imposing barrier?

Early in the 1990s we began to see that providing a safe masculine environment was an essential factor in motivating men to open up to God's transforming power. Based on observation, we have found six basic principles concerning the nature of men that must be respected in order to create a masculine environment:

1. Men respond when their need for space is honored.
2. Men listen when the speaker communicates through questions and answers.
3. Men are goal and challenge oriented. They must be challenged with achievable, bite-size goals and sense an order of progression (one step at a time) in order to achieve those goals.
4. Men are linear in their thinking and tend to focus on either facts or emotions.
5. Men value rules over relationships. They will enter into and develop relationships where structure and freedom are in balance.
6. Men will commit with passion when they are allowed to appropriately express anger and when they learn to express other emotions in a masculine way.

If we desire to see men step back into and engage the church, as well as lead others into the pursuit of God, then we must begin to create a safe masculine context within the local church. When this happens, men will have a place to come home to. They will begin to open their hearts, connect on a deeper level, and ultimately change.

Going Deeper

I believe one of the reasons we typically don't deal with the father vacuum in the church is that there is not a safe enough environment to do so. Many of us have personally experienced this. Let me share a poignant story that has been repeatedly played out in our churches.

Tom's Story

Years ago, I met a young man named Tom when my wife and I became part of a couples group. When Tom was nine years old, his mom and dad divorced. When Tom was fourteen, he became a believer. His dad had extremely high standards of perfection, and Tom struggled with not being able to meet those expectations. He would try for a while, but when he couldn't measure up he'd run–run from his dad and run from the church.

One evening in our couples group he shared his story and laid his wounds open before us. Nobody knew how to respond, though, so they completely ignored what he had shared. Finally, the leader stood up and prayed, and then everyone went home. Tom was left feeling exposed and bleeding.

I was not present, but my wife Jan was, and afterwards, she impressed upon me the need to meet with Tom. I did so, and over the next nine months, in the safety of a masculine relationship, Tom was able to move forward through the process of God's healing in his life.

At the end of the year our small group was doing some self-evaluation, and Tom was very honest. He said, "You left me there bleeding." His perception was that the deep-heart-issues of a man cannot be dealt with in the charged feminine environment of a mixed-gender group.

Bleeding in the Pews

Do you see the importance of safety? If we don't experience safety, we're not going to expose our deep wounds that need to be healed by God. How many men sitting in the pews of your church fit into this category?

Is there a place in the church where Tom and the millions of men like him are able to face the issues of their lives? We must help the church build a safe place where men can heal and become spiritual fathers. We have to create a place that is safe enough for a man to come home to.

I remember sitting in the first Promise Keepers conference in 1991 at Boulder in the basketball arena of the University of Colorado. There were 4,200 guys there that day. I remember being deeply impacted when the men responded so differently than anyone expected. The experts had warned us that men wouldn't touch one another, show emotion, or pray together. But the experts were wrong—men touched one another, prayed together, and showed a broad range of emotion.

I remember leaving and asking myself, *Why was this so different from what I experienced in my local church?* And further, *Why is it so difficult to minister to men?* Over the next two years, God began to open my eyes to many of these issues.

Is Going to Church Like Getting Your Teeth Drilled?

When do you typically decide what you're going to wear to church? When you get out of the shower? A minute before you leave the house? When does your wife decide what she's going to wear to church? An hour before you leave the house? A day before? Some women tell me it's a week before!

By asking these questions, I want to suggest to you that you may treat going to church much like you do going to the dentist. You wake up, clean yourself up, and you leave to take care of your obligation on Sunday morning. But the important question is, *What in this process of church participation do you identify as masculine?* Many men would describe "masculine" activities as hunting, playing sports, watching football, taking a white-water rafting trip, or even playing poker. Whatever you view as a manly activity is part of your identity.

Take a moment and get a visual picture of that activity. When do you start getting ready for it? Isn't it at the very moment you know this activity is going to happen? I can be six months out from going on a hunting expedition in the mountains and I'll mentally prepare myself. So why am I saying all of this? Well, it's important for us to contrast going to church and participating in a masculine activity. Look at the obvious difference: In regard to anything that we view as related to our masculinity, we are there, we are involved, and we are committed to it. But we treat spiritual things like we're getting ready to go to the dentist. We go in, we take care of our obligation, and we get out. Our actions as men are saying, "My identity as a man has nothing to do with my relationships and experiences within the faith community."

Expressing Spiritual Passion

How am I going to be free to express spiritual passion if the environment does not allow me to experience my masculine identity? Without this freedom, how is my family or those around me going to see my passion for Christ? If we want other men to be godly, our own identity as men has to be found in our relationship with God. Then, every person we come in contact with will see our passion for Christ. Would you agree with this theory?

To help men determine whether they are experiencing a safe masculine context within the church, I have asked Christian men from all over the country if they have one close male friend in their church. How many do you think said they have at least one? The results were pretty shocking: approximately five in one hundred. Ninety-five percent of the men I have spoken with did not have one close friend they could call at three o'clock in the morning or go to if they had a moral failure. Only five percent felt that they could safely share their struggles and pain with a close male friend.

The 10:10:80 Principle

The significance of this can be seen in what I refer to as the 10:10:80 principle. When people hear the truth, 10 percent of them change because they're cognitively oriented and the truth changes them, 10 percent never change, and 80 percent change only in the context of a relationship. It's the relationships in our lives that drive us to desire change over time.

Now let's bring these pieces of information together. If 80 percent of the men in the church will only change in the context of a relationship, and 95 percent of them don't have one close friend, how likely are men to change? *The vast majority of men in the church will never change unless something significant changes in the church.*

What are we going to do—continue preaching to the 80 percent, expecting the kind of results you only get from the 10 percent who change readily? If so, we are going to continue to be frustrated by the responses we receive. So why is it so difficult to get men into relationships, and how can we motivate men into relationship with one another so that they can change?

Relationships in a Safe Masculine Environment

We've just illustrated the need for relationships, but it's almost impossible to establish them outside of a safe masculine environment. I saw this clearly demonstrated in the first Promise Keepers conference. Men came into a basketball arena; and even though they might not have been sports enthusiasts, they had all experienced a gym environment and viewed that environment as somewhat masculine. On top of this there were thousands of men laughing and shouting. The atmosphere could have been compared to what you might find at the corner pub or bar with only men present.

The song selection, speaking style, and overall presentation were masculine, and the men immediately opened up. They clearly demonstrated that the experience was a masculine one by making reservations for the following year before they had even returned home from this event. Their actions said, "This connects with my identity as a man."

Six Principles of a Masculine Environment

This leads us to the question *What are the elements of a safe masculine environment?* In my many years of working alongside men, I have found six general principles that depict such a place. They are probably not the only ones, but I believe they are universal in that they effect men from all cultures and are foundational to building men in the church.

Principle #1: Women view closeness as safety and distance as social abandonment; men view space as safety and closeness or intimacy as a threat. When men are threatened they spread out; when women are threatened they come together for security.

I've personally seen this principle lived out in my family and in many others. How will men overcome their fears of being close? Isn't this step imperative towards achieving intimacy?

Carol Gilligan develops this principle in her book, *In a Different Voice: Psychological Theory and Women's Development.* Although I disagree with her pro-abortion stand, Gilligan presents some interesting research on the differences between men and women. She relates a study conducted with groups of men and women where they were shown photographs and asked to share stories related to them. The people in the photographs were either close together physically or farther apart. That was the only difference in the pictures.

The stories the women shared that were elicited by the photographs where people were farther apart contained themes of violence or abandonment. Where the people were closer together, the women's stories pertained to safety and security. When the female researchers listened to the men's stories they were shocked. Their responses were exactly the opposite of the women's: the closer together people were in the pictures, the more violence was in the men's stories; the farther apart people were, the more their stories focused on safety and security.[1]

The Atlanta Olympics

You may remember the scenes on television of the bomb explosion that rocked Centennial Olympic Park at the 1996 Summer Olympics in Atlanta, Georgia. A German film crew had just begun filming an interview with U.S. swimmer Janet Evans when the blast occurred. The event was replayed over and over on the news, and I vividly remember the contrasting reactions of the reporter and the athlete. The male reporter's immediate reaction was to step back from Janet Evans and take a defensive posture by raising his hand with the microphone as if it were a club. Janet Evans, on the other hand, immediately reached for him and tried to move closer. It was amazing to see the interviewer physically move away from others while the female athlete followed her first instinct to seek protection by getting close to another person.

Restroom Space

I want to give you a second example that may be more relatable. Think of the last time you were in a major airport or sports arena and you walked into the men's room. Imagine that there are fifteen urinals in a row and you're the first guy. Where do you go? Typically, you choose one end of the row. Where does the next guy go? Probably as far away from you as he can get. Where does the third fellow go? The middle is usually the chosen spot. The fourth guy has a decision to make and will normally choose a stall!

I was sharing this with some international men one time. A man from New Zealand with his great accent, yelled out, "I know why that is!" I asked, "Well, why is that?" He replied, "When a bloke stands close to you, you have trouble gettin' started." I think there's truth in that.

Again, we force men together—hoping they will open up emotionally. But if men perceive a threat when we try to bring them together with other men, how are we going to address the problem?

The Fear of Small Groups

What happens in church when we try to bring guys together? Don't we tell them to reach across the aisle and hold hands to pray? This is an important step that we would like for men to make, but how do *they* feel about it?

We tell them we're going to place them in small groups with other men, which shouldn't sound too threatening, but that's not what they hear. What they hear is, "We're going to herd you into a room with five men you don't know, you'll have to reveal everything you're struggling with in your life, and then you're going have to focus on those struggles—or *feelings*—for the next year." No wonder they rush for the doors! We have failed to respect the basic nature of men. We need to understand on a deeper level where men are coming from.

I believe the following action points will help create a masculine environment for building relationships.

Application Points:

Give men the freedom to struggle with the process. They are not free, however, to avoid relationships.

- Help men understand that overcoming their fears is essential. They will discover the benefits of developing close relationships with other men over time.
- Have other men function as guides to lead them through their fears. Men who have already experienced this must verbalize and model the journey.
- Set up your facility to honor the principle of a man's space. Choose a room that will accommodate seventy-five men and set it up for fifty. This is close enough for relationship-building but far enough apart for safety.

Principle #2: Women communicate their attention by various listening noises and positive affirmations; men communicate that they are attending or listening by asking questions. Men's questions are usually directed towards trying to solve problems, while women want to be accepted and experience empathy.

We men experience this every day of our lives. If I want to communicate with you, the first thing I'm going to do is ask you a question and you'll give me an answer. You will come back with a question that I can answer in return. Is that the way your wife talks to her friends? It's not the way mine does. She communicates through relating. She uses questions only to identify the subject that she wants to relate on.

Let me further illustrate this with observations of my adult children, Joel and Deb, on the phone. Joel first identified the guy on the other end and then quickly began a rapid-fire question-and-answer volley. "What'd you do today?" "I went fishing." "Where'd you go?" "I went up the Platte River." "Did you catch any fish?" Their conversation continued on and on in this fashion. As soon as one was finished with his interrogation, the other one turned around and followed the same pattern. This is our communication style as men—just give me the facts.

With my daughter, Deb, it was a completely different story. One of her friends might ask her one question, and this lone question would drive their entire conversation. Sometimes a simple, "How are you doing?" could trigger an hour-long discussion. Interestingly, while Deb's friend was talking, Deb would be responding, "Oh, yes, uh-huh, you're right." Those are what I call listening noises—responses that tell her friend that she's interested and involved in the conversation.

Have you ever heard your wife or daughter relate the way Joel did with his buddy? I haven't. In fact, when I try to use that style of communication with Jan, her response is, "Why are you giving me the third degree? What are you doing?"

Men use questions to invite deeper communication.

Questions in Church

Now I want you to view all of this in light of the most critical piece: How often do we communicate that way within the church? How many questions do we make a part of our Sunday morning message?

On one occasion I shared the principles of the masculine context with a group of Hungarian men, primarily by asking them questions. I asked one of the young men, "What happens to you in church?" He answered through the interpreter, "I have trouble paying attention and many times end up falling asleep." To further understand, I asked, "Why didn't you fall asleep tonight?" Interestingly, it was past midnight, he'd been up since five o'clock in the morning, and had been in an intense all-day teaching. He quickly answered, "You asked me questions. I'm thinking about it. It wasn't something you were laying on me. I was engaged in the process of understanding." Do you see the contrast?

In general we are taught in public speaking to communicate in a more feminine style. We're taught to go from global to specific. We're not taught to ask questions. Isn't that interesting? I've personally learned that the more questions I ask, the more effectively I communicate. Some questions don't need answers, some do. But if I can keep asking questions that are relevant to the issue that we're addressing, I can better speak into the lives of those who are listening.

In light of this principle, think back through the discipling materials you've used. Haven't they followed a feminine communication style in that they've asked one question and expected you to relate fully and completely? They might ask, "What is your prayer life like?" How do you answer? "Good" or "OK"? How does your wife answer? She writes a dissertation about how she feels and what answers to prayer she's had.

This principle is progressive in nature. If I was developing a relationship with you, I would move the conversation to the point where you would say, "OK, that's deep enough"; but then in the weeks ahead I would ask you deeper and deeper questions that help move our relationship to the point of better understanding one other.

Application Points:
- Ask a series of open-ended questions that can't be answered by a simple "yes" or "no." This invites discussion and leads to greater understanding and progressive openness.
- To communicate that you are listening when leading a group, you should focus on the responses to your question—not on pushing ahead to the next question. Men will answer questions only when the other men are listening and interested in their input.

Principle #3: Women tend to be security oriented; men tend to be goal or challenge oriented. Men normally see everything around them as a challenge or a goal to be met and/or conquered. In order to feel successful, a man must feel able to control his environment; he will typically look upon situations in his life as obstacles to be conquered. This often causes tension in marriages because the husband is looking for the next challenge while his wife is looking for security. Would you agree?

I have oriented my life from goal to goal, and I'd be surprised if you hadn't done the same. If I were to ask you to think back to when you were twenty-five years old and tell me what your life was focused on, it might take you a while to come up with an answer just because you haven't been there for a while. But I'm pretty sure that you could think back and say, "Well, I wanted to graduate from that college, I wanted to marry this woman, I wanted to get that car, and I wanted this job." Your life was focused on goals. How many of those goals were within the context of the church or your relationship with Christ? I don't believe anyone within the church ever presented to me a clear-cut challenge regarding spiritual goals.

Target Practice

One of my favorite illustrations of how goal oriented men really are came from the *Wall Street Journal* about five years ago. When JFK International Airport in New York was being renovated, the management discovered a big problem with urine on the floor around the urinals and decided that something needed to be done. Their solution was to paint a small fly in each urinal in a strategic spot so that, if targeted, the urine would go where it was supposed to!

Do you see what this says? We're *so* goal oriented that if you give us a target, we can't help but shoot at it! I remember sharing this with a man who said he had just traveled through JFK. I asked, "Well, did you hit the target?" And he said, "Yeah!"

Complementary Elements

I believe that the masculine and feminine elements of goals and security are complementary. The goal to provide for and protect his family drives a man, and his wife's concern for safety balances his drive. Almost every time Jan and I have had significant conflict has been when I've moved towards a new goal in my life. At the time she may have even agreed with me on a decision, but it still undermined her security. Looking back over the years, I can appreciate the balance she has brought to the decision-making process when I've been tempted to take on more than I could handle.

Application Point:

Clearly define a goal or objective that's the right size—large enough to stretch us but small enough that with God's help we can accomplish it.

Principle #4: Women tend to focus on facts AND emotions—they are global and integrated; men tend to focus on facts OR emotions—they are linear and see their world through tunnel vision. Men typically compartmentalize and prioritize, preferring to manage one thing at a time and to look for a specific solution not related to the whole picture.

Cleaning the Coat Closet

One time, when Jan and I were first married, we invited another couple over for dinner. It was July, and we were in one of those hot, dry periods in Colorado when it was about 100 degrees outside. As I arrived home and walked in the front door, I saw that the entire contents of the coat closet had been emptied. I walked up to Jan and said, "What are you doing?" She looked at me like, *Well, you idiot, can't you see that*

I'm cleaning out the coat closet?! Of course, I hadn't asked the question I *wanted* to ask. What was running through my mind was: *It's 100 degrees out, so nobody's going to wear a coat. We've got people coming for dinner, and they'll see the dining room and probably the bathroom. But they're not going to look in the coat closet, so why in the world are you cleaning it out?*

I was looking at the situation as a *man*, but it's important to understand the female mindset. Jan was saying, *I don't care if it's 100 degrees and nobody's going to see the coat closet; if the coat closet is dirty, then the house is dirty—and that's a reflection on me as a woman.* Do you see the difference? Are you still wondering why she was cleaning the coat closet?

Is Communication in the Church Integrated or Linear?

Think again about your experiences in the church. Are sermons and other teachings presented in an integrated or linear manner? Remember what I said before: we've been taught to go from global to specific when we speak publicly. However, men pay attention and listen better when speech goes from specific to global. If I don't connect the dots for them, the global component has no meaning.

I've found that when you speak in a linear (masculine) fashion women always understand your point, although they may think the process is a little boring. But when you speak to men in an integrated (feminine) fashion, they don't even hear it. If I were going to teach a class to pastors on preaching, I would err on the side of speaking in a masculine vein because the women will always hear it anyway.

How many men *want* to be failures? None. Yet we tend to give men in the church lists as long as their arms on how to be godly. When they look at that list and it has twenty-eight points on it, they know they can't do all twenty-eight things perfectly. Giving the man in the pew more goals than he can accomplish will only frustrate him—particularly if, for him, being a godly man requires accomplishing everything on that list. He won't be motivated to do *any* of it. He will sense failure before he has begun. Unfortunately, our tendency in the Christian community has been to heap too many expectations on men all at once.

Application Point:

Give one or two clearly defined steps to help men accomplish a goal.

Principle #5: Women value relationships over rules; men value rules over relationships. Men use rules and structure to produce order so that a situation is comfortable, predictable and non-threatening.

When our kids were younger and they got into trouble, my wife and I had completely different responses. If you have school-age children or you can think back to that time, what did you do when your little boy got into trouble at school? How did you react as a dad? More often than not, I went to him and started asking, "What did you do?" What am I actually asking? *What rule did you break?* What his mother said to him was more like, "How do you feel?" She was more concerned about what the school did to *him*. Do you see the difference? If you put me in a situation like this, I'll always choose rules over relationship.

Why can men play basketball with a group of guys they don't know, who may not even speak the same language? Because we all play by the same rules; we use them to interact with one another, but we don't naturally develop relationships. This enables us to sit by the same man in church week after week and not know anything about him. We may not even know if he's employed or unemployed or if he has a family. Why? Because the unspoken rules that we live by have determined how we interact.

Balancing Rules and Relationships

If we don't develop the right balance between rules and relationships, we won't get through to a man. And if we don't get through to him we will never be able to tap into his spiritual passion. I have found that to do this properly we need enough structure to control the chaos and enough freedom for him to develop relationships. If the situation is total chaos, he won't get involved. If we don't have some structure and subsequent opportunity for freedom through relationships, the 10:10:80 principle indicates that he probably never will change.

Everything we do in ministry to men needs to have enough structure that a man knows why he's attending but enough freedom that, once there, he can develop deeper relationships. If we don't do that, we'll circumvent the process.

It's important to note that many of the current discipling focuses are not very effective because they are highly content oriented. These materials are only effective with men when the "disciples" are allowed to develop a relationship with the "discipler." This relationship is necessary or the disciple will walk away with head knowledge but no heart knowledge. This is why we must have the right balance—enough structure so the man knows why he's there and yet enough freedom to interact beyond a surface level in order to develop a more intimate relationship.

Application Points:
- Create enough structure to control chaos. Men won't get involved in chaotic, threatening situations.
- Allow enough freedom to develop relationships.

Principle #6: Women express a broad range of emotions in a wide variety of ways; men express their emotions primarily through anger. Men need time to process the primary emotions that cause anger.

We're now at the last of the six principles, and I believe that, along with the first one, this may be the most important principle to understand and share with the men in our churches.

The key question for us as men is: *What do we feel the church teaches about anger?* The normal response, and I hear it often, is that anger is sin. If you express your emotions primarily through anger, and you feel that anger is sin, what is that going to do to you? Either you'll put a cork in your anger until it starts to churn in your gut and at some point eventually explodes, or, you'll lock up your emotions inside and take on the demeanor of a passive or dead man, unable to ever express any emotion. In either case, you'll end up emotionally abandoning those around you.

Since we've been told that it's sinful to express anger, we have no way to express it properly. If you put me in a threatening situation or shame me, right away "It's GO time!" (as they say on *Seinfeld*). I won't come back and verbally attack you. I won't sit there and cry. More than likely, I will run.

Anger Is a Secondary Emotion

What do we do about this? It's important to understand that anger is always a secondary emotion. Anger doesn't cause you to be angry. You're angry because you felt hurt, shamed, or frustrated or because you were kept from your goal. So, if you believe that anger is a sin, what does that do to resolve the underlying issues causing the anger? Doesn't it mask them?

If a friend gets angry, I may not want to deal with his anger. But if I really care for him, I need to step into this anger with him and be willing to respond to that anger. Our relationship can afford him the opportunity to get a better understanding of what was causing the anger.

One thing I've realized in my relationship with my wife is that when she's angry she generally knows exactly what she's angry about. She can nail it: "You did this, and I don't like it." I tend to have these confused and discombobulated thoughts—I realize I'm angry, but I'm not sure exactly why. I know what triggered it, but I don't know why I'm angry. Have you ever experienced that? A lot of times it takes a day or two for me to simmer down and pull it all together into something I can understand.

Anger Is Not Sin

If we view anger as sin, we'll never get to what's causing it. We'll end up suppressing it or putting a cork in it. What happens, then, if we don't resolve the issues that caused the anger initially? Anger will rear its ugly head in other places in our lives, seeping out like toxic waste!

We need to correct the misunderstanding about anger. Biblically speaking, anger is not sin. Jesus demonstrated appropriate anger when he chased the money changers out of the temple. In Ephesians 4:26, however, the apostle Paul warned us, "In your anger do not sin." We need to help men find the balance so that their issues can be addressed and resolved in ways that aren't abusive or destructive.

When a man shows anger, the tendency is for others to back away from him because they're threatened. With some training, experience, and maturity, however, we can learn when to stand toe-to-toe and when to move away.

A dear brother of mine, Chuck, and I have this kind of a relationship. Chuck is a retired Army Special Forces lieutenant colonel, and his demeanor at times can be threatening. He's six foot four and goes about 230 pounds. He's a guy who has a lot of energy. But the only men who can speak into Chuck's life are those who are willing to bang foreheads with him. They are the only ones that he respects.

Confronting anger is difficult. Instead of digging in, most men will back off—not wanting to fuel an already volatile situation. It will always be difficult, but we need to allow for it and remember the secondary nature of anger.

Do you see the importance of this? If we're going to deal with men's anger, we've got to have other men who understand the process through personal experience.

Application Points:

Correct the common misunderstanding of anger. Anger is not always sin; it's what we choose to do with it that can lead to sin. "In your anger do not sin …" (Ephesians 4:26).

Create an environment where men are allowed to be angry, but not destructive or abusive in expressing that anger, and where other men understand how to properly react to expressions of anger.

1. When a man expresses anger, we must not recoil nor pursue him immediately.
2. Allow him twenty-four to forty-eight hours processing time so that he will have a better understanding of why he was angry.
3. After allowing time to process, we must come back and try to resolve the issue that caused the anger. We can then take this to the cross to be reconciled.

In reviewing these characteristics, which ones apply to the environment you have experienced in the church? Outside of the church? How important is a safe masculine environment in the church? When you have experienced a masculine environment, do you find it freeing?

Understanding Your Environment

Masculine Characteristics	Feminine Characteristics
Space=Safety	Closeness=Safety
Communicates through questions	Communicates by relating
Goal or challenge oriented	Security oriented
Focuses on facts *or* emotions (Linear)	Focuses on facts *and* emotions (Integrated)
Rules over relationships	Relationships over rules
Emotion expressed through anger	A broad range of emotions

A Disclaimer

Understanding these six principles is important, but I need to share a disclaimer with you: while they are generally true, every man does not express all of them in the same way. Culture plays a significant role in the way men relate and communicate. With this in mind, if some of these principles don't apply to you, be mindful of them anyway because they will be useful on some level for understanding the men in your church. But you don't need to go to the doctor and have your testosterone level checked!

The Bottom Line

Do you see how the principles build upon one another? Men find it difficult to deal with personal issues in the current church context. That's why it's so important to develop an environment within the community of the church that is both safe and masculine. Men need this environment to be motivated to work through the father vacuum and to find a place of comfort when times of crisis occur.

In my neighborhood garages are a big deal. Some even have refrigerators and TVs in them. A number of men have carpeted them and placed their prized possessions (boats, motorcycles, hot rods) in them. If we stand back and look at this phenomenon we might say,

"What about finding a garage or mechanic's shop for men to meet in?" I've had leaders tell me they added on a "working garage" to the church for the men to meet in as well as to serve the widows and single moms in the congregation. I've also heard of churches designing a "bar" setting for their men and going as far as redesigning the men's bathroom with male-focused memorabilia, such as sports pictures and animal heads. The problem is that they can't keep the men out of the bathroom; when the service starts the men are still in there blabbing away!

In spite of some clever ideas, I'm not sure that the physical place is as important as understanding the dynamics and inviting men into a setting within the context of church life where they can feel comfortable and relaxed. It is in this environment that men can let down their guard and start the process of finding their identity within the church community.

A safe masculine environment is absolutely essential in effectively helping men mature from children into spiritual fathers. We need to build it with the minimum amount of structure that allows us to honor the six principles which encourage God's work in the hearts and lives of men.

In order to take the trail leading to spiritual fatherhood we need to have our masculine identity affirmed so that we're confident enough to go where we've never been before. *You have to experience a safe place to offer a safe place.* In the context of this environment you can now experience the process of healing through reconciliation.

---

[i] Carol Gilligan, *In a Different Voice: Psychological Theory and Women's Development* (Cambridge, MA: Harvard University Press, 1982), 40–44.

Chapter 5

What Is Biblical Reconciliation?

The lost man felt safer talking with me than being lost in the woods, but he was unable to trust me (a stranger, and *even worse*, a kid) or benefit from my knowledge of the wilderness. Biblical reconciliation gives men a pathway and process for building trust and restoring relationships so that they are able to find their way out of the wilderness.

The Heart of the Message

Let's start by looking at 2 Corinthians 5:16–20, one of the classic biblical passages on reconciliation. It says:

> So from now on we regard no one from a worldly point of view. Though we once regarded Christ in this way, we do so no longer. Therefore, if anyone is in Christ, he is a new creation; the old has gone; the new has come! All of this is from God, who reconciled us to himself through Christ and gave us the ministry of reconciliation: that God was reconciling the world to himself in Christ, not counting men's sins against them. And he has committed to us the message of reconciliation. We are therefore Christ's ambassadors, as though God were making his appeal through us. We implore you on Christ's behalf: Be reconciled to God.

I believe that this is one of the most powerful yet commonly misunderstood passages in the New Testament. We tend to start out focusing on reconciliation to God through Christ at the cross but quickly move to focusing primarily on racial reconciliation. In saying that, I want to be very clear. The apostle Paul writes, "From now on we regard no one from a worldly point of view." I believe he's saying that reconciliation at the cross demands that I live in reconciliation with every brother. It is never optional. Reconciliation to my brother is a response to my reconciliation at the cross. If I don't live a lifestyle of reconciliation, I'm living in disobedience.

Going Deeper

Parallel passages in Ephesians 2:14 and Galatians 3:28 say that Christ broke down the dividing wall that separated us: Jew and Gentile, slave and free, male and female. Every time we erect one of those walls, what are we doing? It's almost as if we're negating what Christ did. He broke these barriers down. Why are we trying to put them back up? Reconciliation becomes the operating agent in building men. *Reconciliation comes through the cross and is the very mechanism that brings about change. The process of continued reconciliation impacts every area of life.*

The Scope of Reconciliation

We need to look at the scope of reconciliation. First, it starts with God. Without what Christ did on the cross, there would be no possibility of our being reconciled to God or to one another. Yet, we must also become reconciled to ourselves.

I can give you a personal example. I have really long arms. Being in my fifties now, it doesn't make a bit of difference to me; but when I was sixteen it sure did. I was five feet nine inches but my arms spanned six feet one inch. As a member of the human race, my arms *should* span my height. It didn't work that way with me, though. I felt really awkward as a teenager. I walked around and didn't know what to do with my hands. They were down near my thighs and they didn't fit in my pockets well. I could reach down and scratch my knee without bending over! It may sound silly to you, but I believe that one of the impacts of reconciliation to God is that I began to have peace with how he made me.

I'll bet there is something you have struggled with also—whether it's your personal abilities (or inabilities), being an extrovert or introvert, or your image of your body. I want to suggest to you that it's going to be hard for us to reach out and be ambassadors of reconciliation unless we are reconciled to ourselves.

Do you really believe that God didn't make a mistake when he made you the way you are? Do you believe he made a mistake when he brought you through the circumstances of life that you've gone through? God has *always* had a distinct purpose in mind for you.

Being reconciled to God allows me to be reconciled to myself. Being reconciled to myself allows me to be reconciled to my family because I know who I am. The process of becoming reconciled to my family allows me to live reconciled to others. Are we trying to "do" reconciliation instead of living reconciled lives? If so, we disqualify ourselves from being ambassadors because we're trying to "do" reconciliation when the cross has already done this for us. We don't "do" grace—we live in it! We don't "do" justification—we live justified!

What Is Your Comfort Zone?

You have to start this progression in your life to have the full impact of reconciliation. Then it will start to greatly affect every area of your life. Not just a few areas—**every area**. It's going to affect your attitude, it's going to change the environment that you function in, and it's going to compel you to go to people and places, where you wouldn't normally go.

Even though I'm of German descent, I probably never would have ventured into Germany if it hadn't have been for reconciliation. God brought me there and let me experience the common reconciliation of the cross with my German brothers. I began to have more in common with Christian brothers from a foreign culture than with people in my own culture who didn't know Christ. Have you experienced that?

God wants us to be reconciled to his creation, and it's much broader than our own comfort zone. We may have to cross barriers that arise as we pursue reconciliation. Although I am uncomfortable crossing barriers, I want to cross the ones that will lead to relationships. These relationships allow further reconciliation. Do you see the flow of it? Only in the context of relationships can we be ambassadors of reconciliation. Without relationships I violate the whole process and haven't demonstrated being an ambassador of the cross.

Becoming Acquaintances, Friends, Brothers

When I worked with Promise Keepers, I met this feisty Hispanic man—a real character—named Ray. He is probably more different from me than anyone else I know. Normally, we would not have spent a lot of time together, but Ray and I began traveling together in ministry. Can you guess what happened? Because of our mutual desire to be ambassadors of reconciliation, God gave us a unique opportunity to live it out in our relationship.

If you had observed us briefly, you would have noticed a number of differences: he's an extravert, I'm an introvert; he's an American of Hispanic descent, I'm an American of German descent; he was a pastor for seventeen years, I've never been a pastor. However, as we drove across Colorado we began talking about our lives and soon discovered that we had more in common than we had separating us. We had moved from being acquaintances to becoming friends.

An important principle to understand is this: we *compete* where we're *strong*, but we *connect* where we're *weak*. If I try to convince you that I'm strong all the time, what happens to the possibility of our connecting? It sets limits on our relationship and, even further, it places me in a position to compete with you. If I'm going to be an ambassador of Christ and of reconciliation, then I am compelled to demonstrate transparency and expose my weaknesses.

One of the most traumatic events of my life was the death of my two-year-old son, Matthew, in 1978. It began with a call from my wife saying that Matthew was in intensive care at the hospital. The doctors said he had a virus of the heart but he would get better. Later, though, they found that it was a heart defect—similar to muscular dystrophy, except it affected his heart. We took Matthew home from the hospital, and over the next six months we watched his body fail. Finally, we watched God take him home. I was destroyed inside.

I began to share this wounding with Ray. Do you know what happened? We realized that tragedy is not a white issue; it's not a German issue; it's not an Hispanic issue; it's not an African issue—it is a *human* issue. God began to give us a glimpse into the other's heart, the personal journeys we both had been through. And our friendship moved to deeper levels with greater understanding.

Becoming friends with Ray opened my eyes to other painful issues. I began to notice that hotel clerks didn't treat him the same way that they did me, even though we had the same reservation. This relationship caused me to be more aware of other people's pain and wounds.

We can't exhibit Christ's character unless we respond to people the way he did. When the Bible tells the story of the widow who lost her only son, it says that when Jesus saw her, "his heart went out to her" (Luke 7:13). Christ demonstrated compassion. God had moved Ray and me to the point of compassion toward one another, and amazingly, we began to restore respect by the way we responded to one another.

About this time I moved my family to Littleton, Colorado, and a group of men that I had discipled came to help with the move. Ray showed up as well. I didn't ask him to—he just showed up. He was communicating that the differences didn't matter to him any more: "You're my brother, and if you're in need, I'm going to respond to that need."

Not long after this the timing belt on Ray's daughter's car broke, and she didn't have the money to fix it. She needed to get to work, so I replaced the timing belt and didn't give it another thought. Without realizing what was happening, we had affirmed one another. Our actions were saying, "You're valuable to me, you're my brother, and I don't care about this other stuff; if you're in need, I'm going to respond." Do you see what that does? Our actions affirm value and restore respect.

Exposing My Heart

The experiences I had because of my relationship with Ray began to reveal some of the issues of my heart. When somebody cut me off in traffic, I realized I was thinking, "Well, that turkey ..."; and I'd end up having a mental image and verbal comment based upon that person's ethnic origin. Until this point, I wasn't even aware that I was reacting that way.

We don't know what God is going to reveal, but he desires to reveal to us those areas where we're not seeing people the way he does. We must search our hearts for areas where we have not applied his command to view people differently from the way the world views them.

God brought both Ray and me to the point where we both saw "gaps" and knew we needed to ask him for forgiveness. We were then able to move to the point where we could become ambassadors of reconciliation.

The Full Impact of Reconciliation

This illustration of reconciliation between Ray and me was focused on racial reconciliation, but reconciliation is much broader than that. What walls of separation have we erected that Christ died to tear down? Are they denominational? Are they economic? Are they racial? Are they related to age? Where are we separating what God has called into unity? If we're not applying this to every area of our lives, we're not living in reconciliation. We can have programs about it in the church, but we won't see transformation unless people encounter reconciliation by the power of the cross.

If we've never become acquainted, we'll never become friends; and if we're not friends, we'll never be brothers. We have to start the process of letting God break down those walls and take us to the point where we can be used by him to bring unity to the body and see his creative power begin to work in our lives. How do you feel about this? What are the areas in your life that need reconciliation? Are there areas in your life that are out-of-bounds to God? Have you looked at people and thought, "Look at that man ... if he had any willpower he wouldn't be that fat," or, "Look at that guy with the tattoos and earrings. How can he call himself a Christian?" Do you separate yourself from others because of generational stereotypes?

I started to meet with men in 1972 when I began to understand God's calling. On occasion, a new man would come to the men's breakfast and I'd think, *I don't like him.* Invariably, God forced me to love that man. It would have been a lot easier if I hadn't decided beforehand that I didn't like him. I wouldn't have had to go through God grabbing me by the collar and saying, "You're gonna love him!" Prejudice is not necessarily based on the color of skin; I can be equally prejudiced against a brother of my own race if he worships differently than I do. To me, devaluing another person based upon appearance, or something I don't "like," is wickedness from the pit of hell. And it's one way the evil one uses to divide so many of us in the body of Christ.

Where the Rubber Meets the Road

Someone shared a story with me about an elder in a church who was in his seventies. He was an up-front fellow—faithful, loyal, and dependable. His family had been members of the church for quite some time. It wasn't until he entered into reconciliation in the Building Brothers process did this brother communicate his past. He had divorced and remarried, and now had four children with his current wife. They camped together, loved each other, and everything *seemed* great. But his first family was invisible; he had not spoken about them or spoken to them for the past twenty years. No one in the church even knew his first family existed until he joined the men in a Building Brothers group. During the times of interaction in this group, he began to "cough up" his emotions about the anger and unresolved issues.

A young man, the most unlikely individual in his small group, confronted him and challenged him to deal with those issues. In the course of time, the young man was challenged to deal with unresolved issues with his father. Both men were lovingly encouraged in a male fashion to do the right thing and reconcile. Each man received the necessary encouragement and support to experience freedom through reconciliation.

Are there unresolved issues in your life that are keeping God from using you at the level he wants? Are you willing to live with that? Do you want to continue in an unresolved situation that limits what God can do through you?

The Relational Diamond

The pattern of reconciliation follows the same pattern as the relational diamond. Let's apply the progression of the relational diamond to reconciliation.

The relational process and reconciliation start with a commitment to be transformed into Christ's image, allowing us to see people the way Christ sees them. The first step in the process is becoming acquaintances, which involves accepting one another.

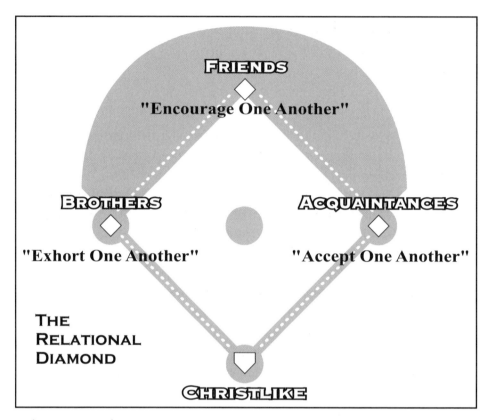

FRIENDS

"Encourage One Another"

BROTHERS

ACQUAINTANCES

"Exhort One Another"

"Accept One Another"

THE
RELATIONAL
DIAMOND

CHRISTLIKE

The "one-anothers"

There are approximately fifty "one-anothers" in the New Testament that were given as commands to believers. You can condense these "one-anothers" into three general categories: we are called to *accept* one another, we are called to *encourage* one another, and we are called to *exhort* one another.

Each "one-another" category represents a corresponding relational level. In becoming acquaintances, we know and accept one another. We become friends as we process through conflict and earn the right to encourage one another. Through encouragement we demonstrate our commitment and we move on to becoming brothers who have the responsibility to exhort one another. Exhortation is encouraging one another to become all that God has called us to be.

A young man once said to me, "You can tell me things that no one else can without me getting angry." I asked him why that was, and he replied, "I think it's because I know you love me." He was saying that we had moved into a brother relationship and we could speak even difficult things to one another.

Journeying Through Conflict

One of the major pitfalls that halts relational growth arises from the principle, *The depth of our relationships, whether with God or with others, will be determined by the level of conflict we are willing to journey through.* If I'm only willing to go through a low level of conflict, this will result in a low level of relationship. In contrast, if I'm willing to persevere through significant conflict I will have a deep and lasting relationship. This is true with friends and family, and it's also true with God.

Conflict is a difficult subject for most Christians. We avoid it and try to get away from it any way we can. But if the depth of our relationships is determined by the level of conflict we're willing to journey through, and we are unwilling to work through conflict—then we are sentencing the church to shallow, ineffective relationships.

I've seen this principle at work in my marriage. The level of conflict we are willing to journey through will determine the depth of our relationships with our wives. The level of conflict we are willing to journey through will determine the depth of our relationships with our sons and daughters as well.

Are we willing to get into relationships and stay in the process until we become transformed into someone God can use? Are you willing to be a servant leader? *It is only as we lead by serving that we will have the credibility to be effective ambassadors of reconciliation.*

Part III

*Building Unity
and Trust*

Chapter 6

What Is the Mandate, Result, and Motivation of Servant Leadership?

Being "found" requires that you trust the one who can lead you out of the woods. The lost man had not been able to observe me over a period of time and test my trustworthiness. It would have taken blind trust or incredible desperation for him to put his trust in someone half his age. What is it that makes us trustworthy and allows others to overcome their fear and follow us? Could it be our willingness to serve them that justifies their trust?

The Heart of the Message

The goal of this chapter is to explain the importance and the impact of biblical servant leadership. To understand this goal one must realize that a repentant *lifestyle* is the foundational character trait necessary to be a servant leader. Repentance is a *lifestyle*, not a one-time act.

We must understand that our assumptions, the preconceived things that we don't even address, generally determine how we lead. We have to expose false assumptions to God's truth and allow them to be changed. Then we will understand how to lead like Christ led. Are you willing to look at and commit to this process?

Going Deeper

A number of years ago I was involved in a Christian organization. We received a report from our insurer stating that more than half of the people in the organization were in counseling due to the intensity and abrasiveness of the organization. What did that say about the organization? How do you accomplish what you've been called to accomplish when you have that many people who are being wounded? If your business is abusing the people who are producing the product that you're going to sell, how are you going to deliver that product?

The "Top Dogs"

It was during that time that God began to work on my heart and took me on a spiritual journey to help understand biblical servant leadership. I want to share that journey with you. While reading in the Gospel of Matthew one morning, I came across a familiar passage in Matthew 20:20–28 where the mother of "Zebedee's sons" (the disciples James and John) approaches Jesus with an unusual request. She asks, "Grant that one of these two sons of mine may sit at your right and the other at your left in your kingdom."

Even though this wasn't the first time I had read this passage, I believe I began to understand it fully for the first time. What was the mother really asking? Who is it that sits on the left and right of the king? The "top dogs"! They're the ones who act on behalf of the king to carry out his bidding; in a sense, they are functioning as kings because they directly represent him. Were James and John naturally in positions of leadership among the apostles? Wasn't their mother asking that her sons be elevated to a position of authority above the other disciples?

In Matthew 20:24, we see that the rest of the apostles hear about and respond to this request. The NIV says that they were "indignant." The word *indignant* is a weak translation. I think they were incensed to the point of rage—if they could've gotten ahold of these two brothers they would have done some serious damage to them. Jesus intervenes and says, "You know that the rulers of the Gentiles lord it over them, and their high officials exercise authority over them."

It was Christ's next words that deeply impacted me: *Not so with you.* What a terse and strong response this was! I'm not aware of any other place in the New Testament where Jesus instructs the apostles in the negative. In the Beatitudes he gives instructions to the masses to help them avoid sin, but with just the apostles his instructions are always in the positive.

Why do you think Christ's instruction here is so important? I believe he is saying to the apostles, "If you even think about leading in this fashion, you should question your commitment to me." It's as if he's saying it's unthinkable and unacceptable that you would ever lead like a king. Why would Christ take this opportunity to single out this one issue and make it a clear, harsh, negative directive?

Leadership Criterion

Jesus goes on to say, "Instead, whoever wants to become great among you must be your servant, and whoever wants to be first must be your slave—just as the Son of Man did not come to be served, but to serve, and to give his life as a ransom for many" (Matthew 20:26–28). It's clear from these verses that we need a new criterion for choosing leadership—a criterion that would determine and underlie the way leaders are chosen. We must choose leaders who have demonstrated servanthood and have a reputation of serving in all areas of everyday life.

Again, God pricked my heart: I could not think of one time in my history in the church that this was the primary criterion that we had used to choose our leaders. We chose men who had abilities, we chose men who had demonstrated charisma, we chose men with money, and we chose men with influence. But we did not choose men who were the best servants in the whole congregation. If we had followed this principle, we probably should have chosen the janitor to be the chairman of the elder board. Can you think of a time in your experience in the church that leaders were chosen on the basis of how well they served? I prayed that God would give me greater understanding about servant leadership and why it is so important.

Saul's Legacy

In answering my prayer, God took me further on this journey. Even though this was not common for me, God began to bring obscure biblical names into my mind. The first name was Mephibosheth. Do you ever have the name Mephibosheth jump into your mind? Do you remember who Mephibosheth was? God had to be doing something, so I grabbed my concordance and looked up every reference to Mephibosheth I could find. I turned to 2 Samuel and began reading about his life.

The first thing I learned was that Mephibosheth was crippled in his feet. When he was five years old, his father, Jonathan, and his grandfather, King Saul, were killed in battle. When Mephibosheth's nurse heard the news, she picked him up and fled—probably fearing for her own life. In her haste she dropped Mephibosheth and his feet were severely injured (2 Samuel 4:4). Isn't it odd that this would be the thing that characterizes Mephibosheth? Nearly every time he is mentioned in Scripture, he is portrayed as crippled in his feet.

I continued to read the accounts of Mephibosheth's life. When King David was well-established in his reign, he remembered his promise to take care of Jonathan's offspring. He searched the land, and the only living relative he found was Mephibosheth. David brought him to his table and restored to him Saul and Jonathan's land and possessions (2 Samuel 9).

Wouldn't you think Mephibosheth would have responded to David like a father? But when David's son, Absalom, rebelled against his father, Mephibosheth apparently also rebelled—although it is not clear whether his servant Ziba deceived him or whether he acted on his own (compare 2 Samuel 16:1–4 and 19:24–30). But Mephibosheth did forfeit his place at David's table and lost the opportunity to be treated as David's son. (And neither Mephibosheth nor any other descendant of Saul ever occupied the throne of Israel.) Could it be that Mephibosheth was not only crippled in his feet but also in his character?

As I pondered this I began to understand—Mephibosheth *is the legacy of King Saul's reign*. The Bible pictures Saul's legacy as defective, damaged, and lasting only one generation. That compelled me to ask this question: What caused Saul to have a legacy that lacked any lasting positive impact?

David's Legacy

Almost immediately another question jumped into my mind: In comparison to Saul's legacy, what was David's legacy? *It is Jesus.* And not only Jesus: through Jesus, David's lineage, *every one of us* as believers has been impacted and brought into God's kingdom. What determines whether a man has a damaged legacy that lasts only one generation or an eternal legacy that has eternal impact?

Facing Tests

I was compelled to look deeper at the contrast between King Saul's and King David's lives. I came to 1 Samuel 24, which recounts the story of David hiding in the cave of En Gedi. Saul had been chasing David to kill him. Needing to relieve himself, Saul happens to go into the same cave David was hiding in, and drops his robe. Rather than listening to his men's encouragement to kill Saul, David instead only cuts off a corner of Saul's robe, and then is immediately conscience-stricken. Why was David conscience-stricken? He realized that he had almost done what only God should do. David understood this because, with his eyes clearly focused upon God, he had the spiritual awareness to sense God's heart. The issue for David was about his obedience to God, not killing Saul—even though Saul was out to kill David.

As Saul comes out of the cave, David confronts him and says, "I have not wronged you, but you are hunting me down to take my life" (1 Samuel 24:11). Knowing that David could have easily killed him but didn't, Saul says, "You are more righteous than I" (verse 17). He goes on further to make an implied commitment to stop pursuing David.

Almost every time I make a commitment to holiness and say, "I'm never going to do that again," I am tested within a short time. Have you experienced this? It's almost guaranteed when those words come out of my mouth that I am going to be tested by that very same issue.

This was soon the case for Saul and David. In 1 Samuel 26 we find Saul once again trying to chase down David, which clearly demonstrates his failure of the test. Likewise, David is also tested with yet another opportunity to take Saul's life. David and Abishai, one of David's mighty men, approach the camp of Saul and his army during the night. Finding Saul and all the soldiers fast asleep, Abishai says to David, "Today God has delivered your enemy into your hands. Now let me pin him to the ground with one thrust of my spear" (1 Samuel 26:8). Abishai was saying, "David, you don't even have to get your hands dirty. I'll take care of this for you once and for all."

David demonstrates that he lived out godly repentance by answering, "Don't destroy him! Who can lay a hand on the LORD's anointed and be guiltless? As surely as the LORD lives, the LORD himself will strike him:

either his time will come and he will die, or he will go into battle and perish" (1 Samuel 26:9–10). David takes Saul's spear and water jug and leaves the camp. David clearly demonstrates he passed his test and that his focus was upon God.

Confession Versus Repentance

Saul's tendency to have his eyes on men and confess rather than repent is further illustrated in 1 Samuel 13. This was early in Saul's reign, when he was preparing to fight the Philistines. Israel's army had gathered and Saul was waiting for the prophet Samuel to come and offer sacrifices, as Samuel had instructed. When Samuel does not come as expected, Saul gets more and more irritated and insecure, and finally, he takes it upon himself to make the sacrifice. Saul directly disobeys the word of the Lord through the prophet of the Lord, so when Samuel arrives he's extremely angry with Saul. Samuel confronts him by saying, "What have you done?" Saul's excuses to Samuel clearly had an underlying theme—he feared the people and what they thought.

God was showing me the primary difference between these two men. Saul was a man of confession; David was a man of repentance. Saul had his eyes upon men; David had his eyes upon God. Do you see the difference?

Repentance at its core is more about *turning to God* than it is about *turning away from sin*. I've spent most of my life misunderstanding repentance: I felt that repentance was when I was caught in a sin and turned away from that sin. True repentance is best modeled by the pattern of the prophet Isaiah in Isaiah 6 when he sees God in the temple. Turning to God and seeing his righteousness reveals our sinfulness and turns us away from sin.

A Repentant Lifestyle

God was showing me one of the root issues I needed to understand about servant leadership. A repentant lifestyle provides the foundation for a man to lead by serving. Only a man who stays humble before God through repentance will be humble enough to be a man who leads by serving. Do you agree with this?

Repentance communicates that you had walked in one direction—away from God—but that you turned 180 degrees back toward God. This is an active, not a passive, lifestyle. I have spent most of my Christian life under the misconception that repentance is only a turning from sin. Biblical repentance at its core is a turning toward God; and as we turn toward him, we turn away from sin—putting it behind us. I focus on God, accepting his gift of grace to me, rather than focusing on my sin and failing efforts to not do "that thing" again.

The picture of Mephibosheth demonstrates that Saul, who was a man of confession alone, could not have an eternal legacy. Only a man who is willing to live a repentant lifestyle where he is continually turning to God will be a man who stays humble enough to lead as a servant. A repentant man is not the controller or owner of the mission, but rather he understands that God has given him a responsibility to serve God's mission. Do you see the contrast?

Two Forms of Leadership

There are two primary forms of leadership: authoritative, controlling leadership and servant leadership. An authoritative leader uses the people to accomplish his goals. A servant leader looks to God and serves the people as they participate in accomplishing God's goals.

As God continued to move me through these issues, another obscure biblical name come into my mind: Rehoboam. Israel's first three kings—Saul, David, and David's son Solomon—ruled over all twelve of Israel's tribes. After Solomon died, his son Rehoboam was immediately accepted by the powerful southern tribe of Judah, because his family belonged to that tribe. In 1 Kings 12, the rest of Israel—that is, the northern tribes—gathered to anoint Rehoboam king. In verse 4, the Israelites opened the dialogue by saying, "Your father put a heavy yoke on us, but now lighten the harsh labor and the heavy yoke he put on us, and we will serve you."

Let's take a moment to try to understand this plea by the people who lived in this small country of Israel. I've been told that the materials that David gathered in preparation for building the temple would be valued at five billion dollars in today's money. We're told that Solomon's palace was even more opulent than God's temple. The people of Israel have just built Solomon's palace and God's temple, and the load on them in conscripted labor and taxes was oppressive. It's no wonder they came to the new king and asked him to lighten the load.

Rehoboam is not an experienced leader, so he seeks the counsel of the elders, or wise men, that had advised his father Solomon. They're old men who have been in service to the king and palace for a long time. They've had access to all the resources of the kingdom and they don't have anything to gain at this point. This was their counsel to Rehoboam: "If you'll give the people a positive answer and *serve* them (the operative word is *serve*), they'll *serve you forever*."

However, Rehoboam immediately rejects this wise counsel and goes to the young men who have grown up with him. It's also important to put these young men in context. These are the men who are going to grasp the resources of the kingdom to build their own houses and personal wealth. They're going to benefit off the backs and through the oppression of the people. These young leaders answer Rehoboam by telling him to say this to the people: "My little finger is thicker than my father's waist. My father laid on you a heavy yoke; I will make it even heavier. My father scourged you with whips; I will scourge you with scorpions" (1 Kings 12:10–11).

Rehoboam accepts this counsel and delivers it to the people, who immediately respond: "What share do we have in David?" The people of the northern tribes reject the Davidic dynasty, proclaiming, "To your tents, O Israel! Look after your own house, O David" (1 Kings 12:16). The passage then ends in verse 19 by declaring, "Israel has been in rebellion against the house of David to this day." Sadly, from this point on, biblical history differentiates between "Judah" and "Israel."

What Do You Want to Produce?

I believe that God was revealing this truth to me: Biblical servant leadership, which is influencing serving leadership, *produces unity and trust*. The gift of wisdom the wise elders offered Rehoboam can be summarized as, "Serve the people and they will trust you enough to serve you in unity." In contrast, controlling, self-serving leadership *produces division, self-interest, and rebellion.* These three results were illustrated by the people's response to Rehoboam.

I was cut to the heart. Do you know why? Growing up in the Denver area I had personal knowledge of and connection with over thirty churches, and I could not think of one of them that had been in existence for at least thirty years that hadn't been through a divisive split or experienced the damage of division. As I reflected on the internal workings of the churches I have been in, I saw that we have been—and still are—full of division, self-interest, and rebellion. How can this be? We were exhibiting the fruits of controlling, king leadership in direct opposition to Christ's instruction to lead as servants. Since we all desired servant leadership, why were we having such a difficult time finding it?

Controlling Leadership		Serving Leadership
Results in:		*Results in:*
Division	————	Unity
Self-interest	————	Service
Rebellion	————	Trust

Every place I visit in the Christian community we are in agreement that we should be servant leaders. I never hear anybody ask for more controlling leadership. We don't need king leadership, someone who will whip things into shape and control every aspect of ministry so we don't have any ownership. Yet, the truth is that much of the fruit of the Christian community is division, self-interest, and rebellion, rather than unity and trust.

Unity in Christ

As I read John 17, the importance of servant leadership became crystal clear to me. This is a familiar passage where Jesus prays for believers, including the believers yet to come. In verse 21 Christ prays, "that all of them may be one …" That means you and me. What does being "one" mean if it doesn't mean that we are in unity? Let's keep going: Jesus prays, "that all of them may be one, Father, just as you are in me and I am in you. May they also be in us …" This gives us a picture of the

Trinity's perfect unity. Jesus continues, "... so that the world may believe that you have sent me." Christ is seen in our culture when he is transparently shown through our unity. When we are in disunity we obscure Christ from the culture and *we participate in sending the people of our culture to hell.* I don't know how that impacts you, but it's hard for me to even say. Could this be the reason we have not seen nation-wide revival in the last hundred years? Unity allows Christ to be seen through his body, the church; and it is unity that draws the culture to him so people clearly see that he's the Savior.

Trust Is Essential

What is it that allows us to trust someone enough to let that person help shape our lives? Why would any rational person follow someone he or she cannot trust? Even if I understand the pathway that calls men into the passionate pursuit of God, but no one can trust me enough to follow me into this pathway, I am going to fail in my service to God and others. Will you follow anyone, anywhere if you don't trust him? Likely you will not. I believe you will have a growing understanding of the importance of trust as you journey through the rest of this section on servant leadership.

Do you remember the passage in Matthew 20 that we looked at in the beginning of this chapter? Christ was saying to the apostles: "The disunity produced by the lack of servant leadership is the very thing that will defeat you. If you lead as kings and set up your own kingdom, that kingdom will be in conflict with God's kingdom and will fall short of carrying out the Great Commission. We must ask two questions: Does my agenda proceed from a desire to build God's kingdom or my kingdom? If it comes from God's kingdom, what method of leadership will help accomplish God's mission?

Can a Program "Produce" Godliness?

When we enter into ministry of any type, it seems that our first instinct is to seek out and select an effective method—a program tool—to reach people with a particular message. However, I believe we need to look at a more fundamental issue: Can any program produce godliness, or can godliness only be reproduced?

In manufacturing, if you find the right process and add the right raw materials, the right product should come out. Similarly, in churches we hope that if we share the right message in a classroom or sanctuary, or use the right discipling tools, people's lives will be transformed. But was that Christ's model as he walked on this earth? His model was one of reproduction rather than production. Jesus lived out everything he said and taught—in every way he was truly the Living Word. While his apostles walked with him over a three-year period, they were impregnated with his words and actions and witnessed firsthand his love for, and obedience to, his Father.

We must be willing to allow God to reproduce his life in us as we commit to walk with him daily. Only when the Living Word has reproduced godly fruit in us can we be used to reproduce it in another. It's then that we can be trusted as leaders and we're able to model and reproduce the passionate pursuit of God. As church leaders, we must focus on consistently living out and affirming the foundational nature of biblical male leadership as well as serving those around us in the church. Through the power of the Holy Spirit, God will use us to transform the lives of others.

Do You Desire to Leave a Legacy?

As men, our impact for the gospel of Christ will be determined by how effectively we serve. Without being servant leaders, we can't accomplish what God has called us to. How can we reach others for God if we don't have the father vacuum filled so that we can pursue him in relationship? If we are not in a safe masculine environment we will not grow and be transformed at the heart level where we can address the issues of servant leadership. If we don't live a lifestyle of repentance we will not stay humble enough to lead by serving.

Do you want to leave a legacy like Saul—damaged, defective, and lasting less than a generation? What kind of man do you desire to be? How can you become a man who is a servant leader and lives a lifestyle of repentance and leaves an eternal legacy like King David?

Identifying Servant Leadership

The following questions will give you, and your leadership team, insight into your effectiveness as servant leaders. Answer the following questions for each of these areas in your life: family, church and business/work.

1. Is the team building leaders or followers? Do leaders come from within or from outside? (Servant leaders build and develop leaders from within and king leaders always build followers.)

2. Does each person in leadership have someone who could step into his position tomorrow if he was to die? (Leaders who are servants prepare others to go beyond them.)

3. Are you experiencing divisive factions within the organization? (Rebellion is difficult, if not impossible, against a servant leader. In contrast, rebellion is almost a guaranteed result of king leadership.)

In order to further develop the character of a servant leader it's necessary for us to look deeper at the repentant lifestyle.

Chapter 7

What Is True Repentance?

To find his way, our lost man needed to turn around and go back to where he had started the day. In order to make it back he would have to see, and understand, where he was in relationship to his camp. I had clearly laid out a path for him to take home, but I wasn't enough of an authority figure for him to trust. He was unable to find a reference point.

God is our authority and reference point. If we are going to be able to turn around and find our way back, we need to see him, and see ourselves in relationship with him, in order to turn from the direction we have been going and follow the trail home. Is God your reference point? Can you be a reference point for others?

The Heart of the Message

Repentance is a lifestyle—not just a one-time act. Repentance is not primarily something we do; it's something we are. We are repentant. We live a repentant lifestyle. Repentance is a progression that starts with seeking and offering ourselves to God, and ends with knowing and doing his will. It can only happen when we approach God from a position of humility and brokenness.

At the most basic level, repentance is more of a turning to God than it is a turning away from sin. It must start by turning to God, since we are incapable of turning away from sin in our own strength. God does the forgiving, the cleansing, the healing, and the transforming—which makes *him* the operating agent. If we orient ourselves to seek God, he does all the rest. We respond to his call and carry out his will only when we're living a repentant lifestyle. Through repentance God becomes our standard and reference point, and we become a reference point for others.

Going Deeper

Let's take a deeper look at the whole issue of repentance. To do this I need to link back to my journey through the Scriptures from the previous chapter. There was an important part that I left out. I mentioned that Saul was a man of confession and David was a man of repentance. Upon deeper reflection, I saw that Saul was focused on men and David was focused on God. It was at this point that I was directed to Isaiah 6, the well-known account of Isaiah's call and commission to be a prophet. I believe this passage gives us the clearest picture of true biblical repentance.

Verse 1 of Isaiah 6 starts, "In the year that King Uzziah died, I saw the Lord seated on a throne, high and exalted, and the train of his robe filled the temple." Do you recall who King Uzziah was? He was a long-reigning king who had spent most of his reign as a godly man. There was a time, however, that he went into the temple and burned incense on the altar of incense—which the law forbids everyone but the priests. The chief priest and eighty other courageous priests took Uzziah to task by harshly confronting him. But the king refused to repent and responded with further arrogance, to the point of raging at the priests. God wasted no time in striking Uzziah with leprosy, and he lived with the disease until his death (2 Chronicles 26:16–21).

A number of Bible commentators feel that Isaiah was related to King Uzziah. It could even be that Uzziah was Isaiah's uncle. Could it be possible that Isaiah was looking to the king of God's people as an intermediary to God? He watched Uzziah go through that period of severe disobedience which resulted in the horrific disease of leprosy. If this was the case, King Uzziah died leaving Isaiah with no one standing between him and God.

In verse 2, Isaiah continues the description of his encounter with God:

> Above him were seraphs, each with six wings: With two wings they covered their faces, with two they covered their feet, and with two they were flying. And they were calling to one another: "Holy, holy, holy is the LORD Almighty; the whole earth is full of his glory."

> At the sound of their voices the doorposts and thresholds

shook and the temple was filled with smoke.

"Woe to me!" I cried. "I am ruined! For I am a man of unclean lips, and I live among a people of unclean lips, and my eyes have seen the King, the LORD Almighty."

Then one of the seraphs flew to me with a live coal in his hand, which he had taken with tongs from the altar. With it he touched my mouth and said, "See, this has touched your lips; your guilt is taken away and your sin atoned for."

Then I heard the voice of the Lord saying, "Whom shall I send? And who will go for us?"

And I said, "Here am I. Send me!"

He said, "Go and tell this people ..."

Seeing God's Holiness and Experiencing Our Sinfulness

For some reason, when King Uzziah was gone, Isaiah was moved to seek God. Could it be that the first step in the process of repentance is to seek God in humility? Whatever is standing between God and us, or being an intermediary between God and us, must first be removed. Isaiah sees God and immediately he experiences his sinfulness. Have you experienced that in your life? Probably the most profound sense of my sinfulness has come when I've experienced God's holiness. Repentance is not experienced when you or I are caught in a sin—it is experienced when we see God's holiness in light of that sin.

Isaiah saw God's holiness, he experienced his own sinfulness, and he realized he was without hope. He expresses that in strong words by saying, "I've seen God; I should be dead, but I'm alive." He was without hope or any recourse. Isaiah throws himself on God's mercy, and one of the seraphs (heavenly beings) flies to him with a coal to touch his lips—in essence, burning the sin out of him.

The pattern of Isaiah 6 reveals the fact that we must humbly throw ourselves on God's grace. There's no hope for you or me in our own strength. Isaiah doesn't say, "I can atone for this. I'll clean myself up and go out and do some good works, and then I'll be acceptable." There is no hope unless God responds with mercy. Our part is to turn to God and experience and acknowledge our sinfulness; his part is to extend grace and to burn sin out of us. Then, like Isaiah, we can answer God's call, and lastly, know God's will. Here are those progressive steps:

Steps in the Progression of Repentance:
1. I need to be humble before God and seek him.
2. I see my sinfulness in God's reflection and acknowledge that I am without hope.
3. I can only throw myself on God's mercy and grace.
4. God burns the sin out of me.
5. I can now answer God's call.
6. I can know God's will.

Notice that Isaiah had to see God, experience God's holiness and his own sinfulness, and *then* throw himself on God's mercy. God burned the sin out of him and he could now answer God's call for his life and clearly know God's will. I have spent a large portion of my life trying to live this progression backwards. My tendency is to begin by saying, "God, show me your will." Implied in that request is my desire to keep control and decide whether or not I want to do his will. If I am comfortable with his answer then maybe I'll cast myself on his mercy, and possibly I'll see his holiness, and maybe I'll focus on humbly seeking him.

In contrast, God's progression of repentance is very clear. God beckons us to come to him and seek him. When we see his holiness, we experience our sinfulness. We then experience his grace. And when the sin has been burned out of us, we can answer his call. Once we have answered his call, the decision is already made to do his will; we commit to his will before we even know what it is.

White-hot Experience
The Voyage of the Dawn Treader, written by C. S. Lewis, provides a clear illustration of the white-hot process of having our sin burned out of us. In this story from *The Chronicles of Narnia* there's this ornery little kid named Eustace who is constantly finding himself in trouble. He ends

up in a dragon's cave, where he looks down and notices he has turned into a dragon and has dragon's skin all over his body. Later on he tries to rid himself of the monstrous skin, but nothing works. He thinks he's finally rid of it only to see that there is another layer that needs to be peeled back.

It's easy to see that we are Eustace and the dragon skin in the story is a picture of the sin in our lives. In the story, Aslan the lion, a picture of Christ, takes his claw and hooks it under Eustace's dragon skin. This painful action splits the skin and it quickly peels away. Later, Eustace exclaims, "When he began pulling the skin off, it hurt worse than anything I've ever felt. The only thing that made me able to bear it was just the pleasure of feeling the stuff peel off."[1] Have you ever had an experience like that? I believe you could say this described Isaiah's experience, and mine as well. *It hurts so bad to have the sin burned out, but it feels so good to have it removed.*

What keeps us from entering this white-hot experience? I remember one time, a few years ago, when I was quiet before God and asked what was standing between him and me. It was as if I could almost see a small word appear: *fear*. I thought, "Fear of what? What do I fear?" God burns the sin out—I can't think of anything more painful than to have somebody take a hot coal and sear my lips. God could have said to Isaiah and me, "You're forgiven." But he didn't do that because we need the experience of having the sin burned out of us. God was showing me that it was my fear of going back into that white-hot place that was standing between him and me. I once heard R. C. Sproul say, "The most terrifying place in the entire world to be is in the presence of God, but it's the safest."

Are You Living in This Pattern?

This same pattern of a lifestyle of repentance is illustrated in various other places in Scripture, each with a slightly different emphasis. For example, Romans 12:1–2 says, "Therefore, I urge you, brothers, in view of God's mercy, to offer your bodies as living sacrifices, holy and pleasing to God—this is your spiritual act of worship. Do not conform any longer to the pattern of this world, but be transformed by the renewing of your mind. Then you will be able to test and approve what God's will is—his good, pleasing and perfect will." Do you see the pattern? I focus on God and present myself to him as a living sacrifice—*before* I know what's coming. God does the transforming and cleansing, and then finally, I know his will.

This pattern of repentance was given to Solomon after he had built and dedicated the temple. In 2 Chronicles 7:14, the Lord revealed the following remedy for times when God's people are in disobedience and experiencing God's judgment: "If my people, who are called by my name, will humble themselves and pray and seek my face and turn from their wicked ways, then will I hear from heaven and will forgive their sin and will heal their land."

Let me help you understand how this has personally affected my life. Most of my existence has been spent with an incomplete understanding of repentance. When I was caught in a sin, I understood that repentance was turning away from that sin. I would say, "I am never going to sin like this again," but would end up being captured by that very same sin. My focus was on my sin and my failure to rid myself of it. Because my understanding of repentance was incomplete, it did not center on God's activity. *It is my turning to God that allows me to see the true depth of my sinfulness and compels me to turn away from my horrific sin.* Do you see the critical difference?

THE Question

The underlying question that plagues us is this: *Is God good and can I trust Him?* I think Isaiah was struggling with this question before he approached God. He had just watched King Uzziah die of leprosy. To watch a once godly Uzziah go through this horrible disease and death must have left Isaiah with questions about God.

Our tendency is to not approach God at a trust level until we are convinced that he's a good Father who can be trusted. For many of us, unhealed wounds from painful experiences with our earthly father can make approaching God or receiving affirmation from him difficult. When we get close enough to God, we will experience and see his goodness and holiness. Seeing his holiness will allow us to more clearly see our sinfulness, and that is the beginning of repentance and transformation.

This connection is even clearer in Romans 12:1–2. This passage focuses us on transformation: "Do not conform any longer to the pattern of the world, but be transformed by the renewing of your mind." The Greek word translated "be transformed" in English is the same word used to describe a caterpillar changing into a butterfly. Repentance is the lifestyle that changes us into something new. Isaiah came out of the process changed—he wasn't the same man. There would be no commissioning of Isaiah to service without this "metamorphosis" into a man who could, with God's power, accomplish his mission and ministry. Yet, many of us are trying to minister without transformation. We are not continually turning to God, and therefore we are ineffective in our ministry

Brokenness Versus Woundedness

You can fake humility, you can fake emotion, you can even fake service to the kingdom, but you can't fake brokenness! A lifestyle of repentance keeps one living in authentic humility produced by brokenness. Frankly, God can't use us fully until we're broken. This means we must be broken to the core and humble enough to serve instead of trying to control God. Do you know what I'm saying? God requires brokenness and humility within us before he can trust us with eternal things. Yet, he invites, and even calls us to this. He has called us to participate in kingdom service which has eternal value.

It's important to note that brokenness means living humbly because of our wounds that have been healed. The majority of society consists of people who are deeply wounded but have never been healed. Sadly, this includes many Christians. They continue to hurt other people as they minister out of the pain of their woundedness instead of out of the humility produced by brokenness. God's healing process that changes woundedness to brokenness is incredibly important.

Do you see the foundational nature of building men who become servant leaders and spiritual fathers? We have to remove the universal barriers that keep men from pursuing God, but if we remove the barriers and we don't call men to seek and see God we haven't accomplished anything. We may have helped them sociologically and psychologically, but we haven't brought them to transformation. We haven't really brought them to the point that they can be spiritual fathers. The call to every believer is to know God's will—it's not optional. The transformational nature of repentance is what allows us to answer God's call and know his will, resulting in opportunities for us to participate with him in what he's doing.

Even though repentance is foundational, men who live a repentant lifestyle don't automatically become servant leaders. We must take time to focus on the personal barriers that keep us from becoming godly servant leaders. Continue with us as we dissect these barriers.

1C. S. Lewis, *The Voyage of the Dawn Treader* (New York: HarperCollins Publisher, 1952), 115–116.

Chapter 8

What Are Your Assumptions in Leadership?

As I sat on the log, the man who was lost stumbled onto me with certain preconceptions about who could help him find his way home. Even though he was lost, it was hard for him to trust someone half his age as an authority figure who could assist him in this journey. Difficult circumstances were bringing him face-to-face with assumptions of leadership that he had never examined, and those very assumptions were keeping him from walking the trail home. Are there unexamined assumptions of leadership that are keeping you from walking on the trail home and leading others on that path?

The Heart of the Message

To this point, I have shared how men have abdicated their role in reproducing a heart for God within the church. We have also looked at the father vacuum and the lack of a safe masculine environment within the church. We have seen how these factors can be major barriers in our personal pursuit of God and in the church's ability to be what God has called it to be. Let's continue to examine what could be the greatest hindrance to the church's impact in the world—the lack of biblical servant leadership.

You may be asking, "Is it really all that important?" *Christ certainly felt it was.* In Matthew 20:25–26, Jesus gives one of the clearest and strongest instructions in the New Testament. In essence, he tells the apostles they are never to lead by "lording it over" people, but that they are to lead by serving, and that they are to choose leaders who have demonstrated by their lives that they are servants. As I look at the Christian community, I see far too few examples of this type of leadership.

Think back to Chapter 6 when we first introduced the following chart, based upon 1 Kings 12:1–19. This chart, contrasting the two different styles of leadership, emphasizes the importance of servant leadership to the church.

Controlling Leadership		Serving Leadership
Results in:		*Results in:*
Division	———	Unity
Self-interest	———	Service
Rebellion	———	Trust

How important is the issue of leadership in the church in a practical sense? George Barna writes, "The church is paralyzed by the absence of godly leadership."[i] Without clearly understanding where the church needs to go and who can take us there, we cannot address the challenges facing the church. As Barna's research demonstrates, the issue of leadership is not seen as very significant by most church leaders: "Only 2 percent of Protestant pastors name personal or lay leadership development, vision clarification and vision communication or strategic development of ministry as top ministry priorities."[ii] In contrast, I would contend that it is critically important that we recognize the need to become servant leaders and reproduce that model of leadership in the church.

Many of us who do desire to be servant leaders are being prohibited by our assumptions of leadership. If we are to change we must examine those assumptions in light of God's model of leadership. *Can we afford to live with the consequences of the status quo?*

Going Deeper

Defining Biblical Leadership

Without a clear definition of biblical leadership, how can you call somebody to follow you and live as a servant leader? I want to propose a working definition of biblical leadership: *effectively influencing others for the kingdom of God.* Would you agree that this is an acceptable definition?

To further understand the definition of biblical leadership, we must ask the question: *What's the mission of biblical leadership?* Clearly the mission for biblical leaders is to be part of building the kingdom of God. Do we need to control people to accomplish this mission? Should we try to force or manipulate them into the kingdom? My experience in the church would lead me to believe that we typically would subconsciously answer "yes" to these questions. If we see our mission as "putting butts in the seats," then we will use whatever methods are available to make that happen. (If your job security depends upon attendance numbers, that is exactly what you must do.) If our mission is to effectively influence others for the kingdom of God, then we must change our methods and our definition of leadership.

Influence Is Not Control

It's important to look at each of the key elements of our definition. The best way to understand influence is to understand what it is not. Influence is not control. It isn't about using other people.

If we agree that servant leadership is what we are called to, then why do so few live it out? If you're like me, you have a real desire to live for God and yet you still struggle with the tendency to control as a leader. What happens when our leadership is attacked? We feel threatened by the attack and will typically protect our "position." The key question is *Whose kingdom is it*? Is it mine, or is it God's? If it's mine, I'm going to defend it with all the ammunition that is necessary. If it's God's, he will defend it and I can relax my control.

A Stark Contrast

In 1997 I was traveling to Texas at the time Princess Diana died. Then, within a few days following her death, Mother Teresa died. I was interacting with many Christian people at that time, and I watched their responses to these two deaths. They were enthralled about Princess Diana and talked about it continuously, but when Mother Teresa died they were baffled as to how to respond.

As I pondered this, I began to understand their response. Many wanted to be like Princess Diana—wanting to be a prince or princess or a king or queen, living in the palace and every once in a while stepping out of the palace and touching the people of their kingdom. Once this "charity" work was done, they could go back behind the walls to the privileges of the palace.

I really don't think we know what to do with someone like Mother Teresa who rejects a life of privilege and comfort. She was the daughter of a Yugoslavian duke, which made her royalty. Her early years of life were privileged, but she stepped out of that life and never went back. What would motivate her to make this choice and stick with it? Most of us would struggle with leaving our position of privilege and power to live with and influence others.

Wanting To Be King

I struggle with this myself. Do you? My natural tendency is to assume that in order to have significant influence I must have position, privilege, and power. In Matthew 20:20–21, what did the mother of Zebedee's sons want for her boys? She wanted them to ride first class and be elevated like kings. This reveals something about her assumptions, which Jesus immediately corrected. She assumed that the nature of leadership is to be in a position of power. In contrast, Christ establishes that the nature of leadership is to accept the responsibility of serving. *It is when we serve that we have the opportunity to influence.*

Why is it that we in the Christian community struggle with this issue of wanting to be kings? Our temptation is to try to give the appearance of doing good works and being servants while not giving up any position of privilege and power. It is through serving—extending love and influencing others—that we attain the result of Christian leadership.

Popular Leadership	Biblical Leadership
Controlling through:	*Serving through:*
Position ———	Calling
Privilege ———	Responsibility
Power ———	Influence

Is Christian Leadership "Anointed Leadership"?

Popular or controlling leadership is often justified by accepting the principle of "anointing" to a position of leadership. How does anointing relate to leadership? In the Christian community do we feel our leaders are anointed to the position of leadership? As a leader, if I believe that leadership is an anointed position, does that give me the right to my leadership position? In the Old Testament it did. In the Old Testament there were three anointed positions: prophet, priest, and king. The anointing gave you responsibility and the right to power and position.

As Christians, many of us assume that if we're in a position of leadership we have a right to the privileges of leadership. In trying to understand the nature of leadership, I searched the New Testament for every reference to *anointing* in order to see if leadership is described as an anointed position. I only found four references where some form of the word *anointing* was tied to leadership. Every passage referred to Christ being anointed to be *the* King and that his is the only kingdom. That really intrigued me.

I expanded my search to other leadership positions by searching words such as *overseer*, *pastor* and *elder*. Again, there were no references that tied anointing to New Testament leadership positions. The New Testament never uses the word *anointing* to describe positions of leadership. The nature of leadership is a "calling." The King James Version describes the calling to leadership as being "sanctified" or "set apart." The two terms mean the same thing: to be called is to be sanctified—set apart—for a special purpose of service.

Do you see the contrast? If I see leadership in the pattern of the Old Testament model, then I have a right to be the king. If I accept the New Testament model of leadership that Christ gave us in Matthew 20:25–26, then I am called and set apart to serve a group of people.

The New Testament clearly teaches that there is an anointing of God's power in order to accomplish God's work. However, the danger is seeing the *position* of leadership as anointed, thus, almost guaranteeing the abuse of the people we are called to serve. Many of us view leadership in our churches as anointed positions. This view carries dangerous DNA into the church. If you attack my leadership position you're attacking my anointing; my natural response is to exert control over the situation and protect my rights as a king. Could this be the cause of many of the abuses we are struggling with in the church today?

Are Influencers Leaders?

As you look back, what person(s) had the most impact on your life? Who influenced you the most: your dad, your mom, a pastor, a teacher, a coach, a commanding officer? A number of years ago, I asked a group of men that same question. After they identified a specific person, I asked them to identify the personal characteristics that allowed that person to influence them. Was it their commitment, integrity, passion, desire to serve? The men identified the following personal characteristics of those who had the greatest influence in their lives: they served others, demonstrated integrity, were humble, showed self-confidence, demonstrated passion, had strong beliefs, showed compassion, were accepting rather than judging, and demonstrated personal strength.

I took it one step further and asked, "Was that person a leader?" They quickly answered no. Amazingly, they did not perceive the person who had influenced them the most to be a leader. This revealed a common assumption that a leader is someone who controls through position, not someone who serves through influence. Do you see how important this is? If I assume that the role of a leader is to control, then when I am pressured as a leader I am going to control. If it is my perception that influencers are not leaders, I won't get the full benefit of their leadership.

Servant Leader Versus King Leader

As an influencing servant leader, I serve through my calling, accepting the responsibility and influencing people effectively for God's kingdom. As a controlling king leader, I use my position, privilege, and power to guard my position and protect and advance *my* kingdom. Do our efforts to control demonstrate a desire to be God or usurp God's role?

In mathematics, what happens if your assumptions are wrong? No matter how accurately you follow the process, you are going to get the wrong answer. The same is true with leadership. If we're functioning with incorrect assumptions, even though we're trying to be servant leaders, we are not going to end up with the result that we desire.

A friend of mine who had been a senior pastor shared his story with me. He had led his church as a servant but had come to a financial challenge. He felt the need to follow the common pattern and find a well-known pastor/authoritarian leader and put him in charge in order to raise money and take the church to the next level. This new pastor led out of position, privilege and power, and destroyed the servant/influencing dynamic of the church. Why? Because he assumed that he needed control in order to accomplish the vision. Many of us get to a certain point in our lives by serving, and then—even though God has been blessing us—we say, like the children of Israel said, "We need a king."

This same principle happens in the business world. I have a good friend who started a corporation. At one point his stock in that privately held corporation was worth $62 million. All the experts were telling him he needed to take the company public so that he could take advantage of an expanding market. He felt God had clearly told him he was never to do that, but he finally gave in to the assumptions of the experts. His stock is not worth a dime today. This is his evaluation of that decision, "I was disobedient to God by desiring an earthly king. I had been able to take the company this far by trusting God, but I felt inadequate in my own abilities and went and got an expert, a king, to take us to the next level. That was the beginning of the end."

The Importance of Examining Our Assumptions

We must understand and address our own assumptions in order to be able to appropriately submit to leadership and participate in leadership. The fact that many of us carry false assumptions that have never been exposed to the truth of God's Word will destine us to lead in a defensive and destructive fashion. Do you see how our assumptions will determine how we choose leaders and how we lead others?

It's critical that we understand the assumptions that build our foundation of personal leadership. After we allow God to correct our assumptions, we will begin to lead in the way Christ called us to lead. In this chapter I have attempted to expose some of the universal assumptions that must be examined to start that process. As you read through the chapter, did you identify some false assumptions that you have learned from those who modeled leadership for you? It is time to begin to replace those assumptions with the truth of Christ's model of leadership. We will continue to further examine and understand Christ's model of leadership in the chapters to come.

1 George Barna, *The Second Coming of the Church* (Nashville: Word Publishing, 1998), p 101.

2 George Barna and Mark Hatch, *Boiling Point: It Only Takes One Degree* (Ventura, CA: Regal Books, 2001), p 246.

Chapter 9

What Was Christ's Model of Leadership?

When someone is lost, their ability to be "found" or "find their way" will depend upon the patterns they learned before they discovered that they were lost. If their patterns are inadequate it is essential that someone help them find their way. In my interaction with the lost man I was trying to establish a progressive process to help him find where he was and locate his camp. In similar fashion, in Luke 10 Christ gives us a clear roadmap showing how to lead others to where they need to go.

The Heart of the Message

A person's history of serving is the main qualifier Christ gave in selecting leaders (Matthew 20:25–26). Could it be that those in church leadership need to return to Christ's basic standard for choosing leadership in order to address the crisis in the church today?

In manufacturing, if you find the right process and add the right raw materials, the right product should come out. Based on this knowledge, those of us in leadership hope that if we share the right message in a classroom or sanctuary, or use the right discipling program, men's lives will be changed and godly leaders will be the result. But was this Jesus' model? His model was one of reproduction, where he lived out what he wanted to be reproduced in his disciples. In every way, he became the Living Word. While his disciples walked with him over a three-year period, his words, actions and character were formed in them. After his resurrection, the disciples became, in a very real sense, Christ to the church.

What the church needs now is a change in the way it views leadership—that is, apart from selfish ambition or pride. Biblical leadership must be viewed through the lens of Christlike servanthood. Men must step forward and accept the call to leadership with their eyes fixed on Christ and a desire to serve others. To accomplish this, men must come together in relationship with one another, as Christ did with his disciples, and model what it means to pursue God and live for him.

It has been said that *we teach what we know but we reproduce what we are.* As leaders, we must be willing to allow God to reproduce his life in us so we can be used to reproduce his heart in others. Only when the Holy Spirit has reproduced a passion for God in us can we be fully used as messengers of God's love to others.

Going Deeper
Christ Models Servant Leadership as He Sends Out the Seventy-Two

One of the clearest examples of Christ's model of servant leadership can be found in Luke 10. This is where he sends seventy-two of his followers out to heal the sick and tell the people about the kingdom:

> After this the Lord appointed seventy-two others and sent them two by two ahead of him to every town and place where he was about to go. He told them, "The harvest is plentiful, but the workers are few. Ask the Lord of the harvest, therefore, to send out workers into his harvest field. Go! I am sending you out like lambs among wolves. Do not take a purse or bag or sandals; and do not greet anyone on the road.
>
> "When you enter a house, first say, 'Peace to this house.' If a man of peace is there, your peace will rest on him; if not, it will return to you. Stay in that house, eating and drinking whatever they give you, for the worker deserves his wages. Do not move around from house to house.
>
> "When you enter a town and are welcomed, eat what is set before you. Heal the sick who are there and tell them, 'The kingdom of God is near you.' But when you enter a town and are not welcomed, go into its streets and say, 'Even the dust of your town that sticks to our

feet we wipe off against you. Yet be sure of this: The kingdom of God is near.' I tell you, it will be more bearable on that day for Sodom than for that town. ...

"He who listens to you listens to me; he who rejects you rejects me; but he who rejects me rejects him who sent me."

The seventy-two returned with joy and said, "Lord, even the demons submit to us in your name."

He replied, "I saw Satan fall like lightning from heaven. I have given you authority to trample on snakes and scorpions and to overcome all the power of the enemy; nothing will harm you. However, do not rejoice that the spirits submit to you, but rejoice that your names are written in heaven." (Luke 10:1–12, 16–20)

Seven Principles of Servant Leadership

I want to suggest to you that there are seven principles of leadership that Jesus illustrates in this passage and in Matthew 20:25–26.

1. *Honor those above you and focus on those who are positioned below you.*

    If you follow Christ's model you will always focus on those who are positioned below you rather than on those who are above you. A servant leader always has a view down through the people who are accomplishing the mission. When a king leader has a position of authority, he uses those below him to accomplish the goals of those above him. Have you experienced this? It's clear in Matthew 20:25–26 that this is not Christ's model: his view is right down through all levels of leadership, ending at the person who is carrying out the mission on the street.
    Reflection Questions: Do you know the needs of the people you are leading? Knowing their needs is evidence of a downward view. Do you honor and show respect to the people to whom you are accountable?

2. *Clearly communicate the mission and "give it away."*

    Christ communicates the mission in Luke 10:9 by telling his disciples to heal the sick and announce the kingdom of God. The mission was clear; and it is not only *his* mission, but it becomes their mission.

    Reflection Questions: Do those you are leading understand the mission? Have they internalized it? Are they sharing the mission with others and are they starting to attempt to accomplish the mission even when you aren't around?

3. *Set clear parameters that those you lead are free to function within.*

    This principle can be seen in Luke 10:1–7. A servant leader always sets clear parameters that the people he leads can func tion within. There are two focuses for those parameters. First, you identify pitfalls that will cause them to fail. Jesus said, "The harvest is plentiful, but the workers are few. Ask the Lord of the harvest, therefore, to send out workers into his harvest field." I believe Jesus was saying, "You can't accomplish this task—only God can do it. The workers are few, so *trust in him* to accom plish it." Now let's look at the next verse: "Go! I am sending you out like lambs among wolves." Isn't Jesus saying that we can't protect ourselves? "If you try this in your own strength, you will get caught up trying to protect yourself and never accomplish what I've sent you to do."

    But there is a second focus that is often missed: Jesus clearly identifies their responsibility and authority. The responsibility he gives them is limited to the mission, which is to heal the sick and to announce the kingdom. What is their authority? In reality it is his authority. He says, "He who listens to you listens to me; he who rejects you rejects me." He gives limited responsibility along with authority that is in excess of what is needed to accomplish the task.

    My personal tendency, and the tendency I see in the church, is to do the opposite. We say, "Go change the world, but before

you do anything significant come back and check in with me."
We haven't matched the responsibility and the authority. If I lead
in this fashion, I have cut your legs off at the knees and stymied
your progress, because I haven't given you the freedom and
resources to accomplish the mission. Have you experienced this
in the church?

We must follow Christ's model. First, we must identify the pit
falls that would keep those we lead from being successful.
Second, we need to give limited responsibility matched with
authority that is in excess of what is needed to accomplish the
mission.

Reflection Questions: Are the responsibilities of the people
you're leading clear? Have they been given enough authority to
accomplish the mission? Are your guidelines keeping them from
common pitfalls?

4. *Release those you lead to accomplish the mission.*

We need to let go of the control of the people under us so they
can accomplish the mission. Jesus didn't send the seventy-two
out to the surrounding towns and say, "I'm going to come and
critique you. You go to one house; I'll watch what you do and
I'll tell you what you did wrong." If we do our job correctly as
leaders—communicate the vision, give clear parameters by identi
fying the pitfalls and delineating clear responsibility and proper
authority—then we don't need to critique and control every
action. Like Christ, we should release them in a fashion that frees
them to accomplish the mission.

Reflection Questions: Do those you lead feel free to move
ahead and accomplish the mission? Are they functioning, the
majority of the time, at a level where they feel free to act and
later inform you of their progress? Are they exhibiting confidence
in knowing where they are going?

5. *Watch the process in order to remove roadblocks that those
    you lead cannot remove.*

Jesus was watching for obstacles the disciples wouldn't be able to overcome and removed them before they caused the disciples to fail. We see the evidence of this in verse 17, when the seventy-two complete their mission and report, "Lord, even the demons submit to us in your name." Who gave the authority to remove the demons when they came up against them? Christ did. Had they been told to cast out demons? Not in this passage. They were told to heal the sick and announce the kingdom. Removing the demons was a roadblock they came up against. Jesus watched the process and gave them the power to remove the roadblock, which gave them freedom to grow. As a general rule, if we follow Christ's model it will be known that we've removed the roadblock.

Reflection Questions: Do those you lead always run back to you with a crisis you must deal with? Are you anticipating and addressing most roadblocks before they reach them? Are you regularly praying for them as they are carrying out the mission?

6. *Celebrate the victories of those you lead.*

When the seventy-two returned with joy and shared that even the demons submitted to them, Jesus replied, "I saw Satan fall like lightning from heaven." It was as if he was saying, "Wow, look at that! My sons overcame, and because of this Satan fell from the sky like a star from heaven." Jesus revels in celebration with the disciples. This was not the time to critique them. Nor did he focus on his part in accomplishing the victory.

I personally struggle with this step the most. My northern European-German heritage comes out and I do not celebrate very well. I always want to go to my son when he does something and say, "Joel, you did a good job, but this is what you could have done better." Do you catch yourself doing that as a father? Do you see this within the church? In using "but ...," I have destroyed any possibility of authentic celebration. I leave those

I'm leading feeling like they didn't really accomplish the task as well as they should have, or, as well as I would have.

We don't see Christ doing this. He could have said to the seventy-two, "Don't you understand that it was *my* power that allowed you to cast the demons out? It was really *me* who did it." But He didn't. When those we are leading are successful, we need to celebrate with them with no correction, with no "but ..."; we need to focus on and celebrate what's been accomplished.

Reflection Question: Are you leading the celebration when those you lead are victorious?

7. *Focus those you lead on who they are—not what they do.*

When the celebration has died down we are given a perfect opportunity to reaffirm their identity in Christ: *what they do is not nearly as important as who they are.* What they do should flow out of who they are as sons of God. Jesus said to the seventy-two, "Do not rejoice that the spirits submit to you, but rejoice that your names are written in heaven." In the most practical terms he was saying, "Don't focus on what you do; focus on who you are!"

If we focus on what we do, we'll lose our ability to do it. What I do doesn't make me who I am; it's a reflection of who I am. Every Christian organization that I'm aware of that has failed has done so because they ignored this principle. They began to focus on the dynamic of what they did and that allowed them to lose focus on who they were in Christ. This brought them to the point of failure and ultimately destroyed their ability to complete their mission.

Reflection Question: Are you pointing those you lead back to their identity in Christ?

How To Best Apply These Seven Principles

If it was difficult for you to answer the question(s) following a particular principle, that principle is one you need to focus on in order to lead as a servant. Because each principle builds upon those that precede it, a shortfall in one will affect all the others. Most men find it is easier to be a servant leader in their vocational life than in their family life. God's truth needs to infiltrate every area of our lives.

The Transformational Environment

Romans 12:2 says, "Do not conform any longer to the pattern of this world, but be *transformed* by the renewing of your mind. Then you will be able to test and approve what God's will is—his good, pleasing and perfect will."

In the church there are two types of relational climates. One relational climate is the *transformational* environment; the other is the *controlling* environment. The first will free a man to reach his spiritual potential, while the second constricts and stifles spiritual growth. Servant leadership produces a transformational environment. Christ's pattern of leadership, used to build leaders, was servant leadership. It was on this model that he founded his church. He created a transformational environment that allowed the disciples to mature into their calling as apostles.

In order to help men enter into the passionate pursuit of God, a transformational environment must be created. In many churches the current environment is controlling rather than transforming. A transformational environment is essential for men to mature into spiritual fathers. A conforming and controlling environment will imprison men where they are and keep them from freeing others to be all that they can be.

The following chart illustrates the contrasts between the transformational and controlling environments. Which environment do you want your leadership to create.

Contrasting Environments

Controlling Environment		Transforming Environment
Finding Blame	vs.	Finding solutions
Appearance	vs.	Substance
Condemning	vs.	Confirming
Untouchable issues	vs.	Open discussion
Criticizing	vs.	Encouraging
Stereotyped roles	vs.	Flexible roles
Valued for what you do	vs.	Valued for who you are
Resitant to change	vs.	Free to grow
Depletes personal value	vs.	Builds personal value
Restricting	vs.	Releasing

Focus on each contrasting pair one at a time. On the left side, you're going to find the characteristics of a controlling environment produced by authoritarian king leadership. On the right side, you will find the characteristics of the transformational environment produced by biblical servant leadership.

As you evaluate each pair, answer the following question: Which characteristic do you want to characterize your family, your church and your workplace?

The Relationship Between Spiritual Fatherhood and Servant Leadership

Spiritual fatherhood is based on servant leadership. These seven servant leadership principles are the same ones we need to use as spiritual fathers. We need to help our spiritual children understand their mission, release them, let them make a few mistakes, come alongside and remove the roadblocks, celebrate with them, and most importantly, bring them back to the reality of who they are in Christ. We must begin to build leaders in the church: men who are—in their pursuit of God—becoming reproducing spiritual fathers.

Do you see the journey we have taken in this section on servant leadership? We've gone from the importance of being servant leaders, to the foundational issue of repentance that transforms our character, to our false assumptions that will defeat us, to Christ's model that empowers us. Now it's time to move on to the transformational environment that is produced when we lead by serving. In order to stay committed to servant leadership it is critical that you and I understand the kind of environment we will produce when we are servant leaders.

God is calling each of us to begin the process of maturing from spiritual childhood to spiritual fatherhood. Spiritual fatherhood is characterized by reproducing succeeding generations of spiritual fathers. It is critically important for us to understand that reproduction is the process. In order to accomplish this we must be servant leaders who are demonstrating that we can be trusted because of Christ who dwells within us. Then, other men will be able to follow us into this process. In the next chapter we will examine the process of spiritual reproduction.

Chapter 10

Are You an Instrument of Spiritual Reproduction?

As I stood on that hillside in Colorado so many years ago, I didn't understand that I needed to reproduce my confidence and ability to orient myself within the lost man or he was not going to be able to make good use of the resource that I could be to him. As it was, he could only trust me to get him back to a trail that he had walked before.

Could it be that, unless we can reproduce a passion and pathway for the men of the church we will send them back to walk the destructive trails that they have walked again and again?

The Heart of the Message

It is through our creative, reproductive nature that we are driven to seek significance.

We, as men, desire more than anything else to create a legacy and make our lives count by leaving something that is lasting. We try to fulfill this desire in many ways, not the least of which is physical reproduction. It seems clear that God uses the pattern of our physical reproductive nature to help us understand spiritual reproduction. God is calling men to spiritual reproduction.

In the New Testament it is no longer the physical act of circumcision that marks the people of God, but the spiritual "circumcision of the heart." Romans 2:28–29 and Colossians 2:9–13 tell us that this circumcision of the heart is accomplished by the Holy Spirit and this marks the believer. Our identity is found in Christ, so we make a choice every day to walk as men of the new covenant; and we reveal this choice to everyone we encounter. Are you willing to live out your pursuit of

God so that others see your heart and want to follow?

Since we are born again through the Holy Spirit, we carry the imprint of God—and he makes us a new creation. "He anointed us, set his seal of ownership on us, and put his Spirit in our hearts as a deposit" (2 Corinthians 1:22). "Therefore, if anyone is in Christ, he is a new creation; the old has gone, the new has come!" (2 Corinthians 5:17).

In the past century we have had more learning tools and programs available to the church than at any other time in our history, but the church continues to be diminished in its impact on our culture and the world. We continue to put our efforts into finding the right tool or program to produce godly people. If the statement, "We teach what we know but we reproduce what we are," is true, then our dilemma is primarily that we are not what we need to be in order to reproduce what we should. We must ask God to begin working within each one of us in order to see a strong, vibrant model of godliness emerge from the church—a model developed first within a core of leaders who desire to be the firstfruits of what God wants his church to be.

Going Deeper

Physical Circumcision

At a men's conference a number of years ago in which I was speaking, the first speaker began by teaching from an obscure passage in Joshua 5 concerning the circumcision of the men and boys who had been born during Israel's forty years in the desert. The passage recounts what happens when Joshua realizes none of the Israelites born in the wilderness had been circumcised. Before going into the Promised Land, God required that they be consecrated through circumcision according to the covenant he had made with Abraham. The place where all these Israelites were circumcised came to be known as a "mountain of foreskins" or a "hill of foreskins." The speaker concluded with a challenge to the men at the conference to consecrate themselves to God, turn away from sin, and get ready for battle.

My mind began to race while he was preaching—why had God chosen circumcision as the mark to signify his covenant with

Abraham and his descendants? Any mark would have consecrated the person, so why had he not chosen a more conspicuous area of the body? Why would he choose something as intimate and private as the penis? It occurred to me that only through the ritual of circumcision, when the member or instrument of a man's reproduction was consecrated, would God then have the whole man consecrated to him. Even further, when he had the whole man, he would then have the family—the foundation of the entire nation—fully consecrated to him.

Circumcision of the Heart

I began to think of Romans 2:28–29 and Colossians 2:9–13, where the Scripture talks about the circumcision of the heart. In the Old Testament, God called for the circumcision of the physical member, the penis. In the New Testament, it is no longer the physical act of circumcision that marks the people of God but the spiritual circumcision of the heart. Circumcision of the heart involves the very core of a man and allows us to express the power of God through participating in spiritual procreation.

In essence, Paul is saying that we have become *the instruments of reproduction.* Now, I know this may make you feel a bit uncomfortable (as it does me), but God wants us to become an instrument of spiritual reproduction, fully consecrated to him. So he circumcises the heart, the core of our being, enabling us to bear spiritual offspring. Our search for significance can only be accomplished through becoming spiritual fathers who reproduce spiritual fathers and mothers.

Physical Versus Spiritual Reproduction

Let's examine the elements of physical reproduction and parallel them with spiritual reproduction. Physical reproduction starts with the seed, which carries the father's DNA. It must unite with the egg, which carries the mother's DNA, in order to reproduce new life. The child will inherit the traits passed on by his or her parents. So it is in the spiritual realm as well, as illustrated by Jesus' words to Nicodemus: "I tell you the truth, no one can see the kingdom of God unless he is born again ... Flesh gives birth to flesh, but the Spirit gives birth to spirit" (John 3:3,6).

Am I Fertile?

In spiritual reproduction, as in physical reproduction, the DNA doesn't come from us; it comes *through* us and *from* God. So, the first question is, "Am I fertile?" I can only reproduce what I am, so if I don't have passion for God, and if I don't really know him on a deep level, then I'm unable to be used to reproduce his love in anyone else.

Am I Potent?

An excitement stirs our own spirits when we are around others who are passionately pursuing a personal relationship with God—this is the DNA. We can only accomplish our role as an instrument of reproduction when we've "caught" this passion and are capable of being used by God. I must ask the question, "Am I potent?"—because I must be a willing and able instrument, ready to be used in the process of spiritual reproduction.

Am I Practicing Spiritual Birth Control?

The next question I need to ask is, "Am I practicing spiritual birth control?" If I am fertile and potent, what is keeping the DNA from achieving implantation so it can create new life? There are many influences that can hinder, obstruct, or halt the process of spiritual reproduction. At times within the church we are practicing the equivalent of spiritual mutual masturbation. We spend a lot of time gratifying one another, but we're not accomplishing reproduction. Our ability to reproduce the Christian life proves fruitless because of unconfessed sin, lack of healing or disobedience. We must allow confession, repentance, and forgiveness to wash us clean and free us to approach again the throne of grace.

Intimacy Is Imperative

If I'm fertile, and potent, and I'm not practicing spiritual birth control, then the necessary environment of reproduction is intimacy. This intimacy can be defined as a relationship with God and with those whom we are to be used to help reproduce a Godly passionate relationship with. We often try to achieve reproduction from a production method without the significant level of intimacy that's required. We demonstrate that we are committed to a production method by saying, "Just use this resource and *it* will transform you and make you a committed believer." I have rarely seen this method work. There are times when God miraculously works in the lives of people and "jumps" them forward in their faith, but this is not the norm for 99.9 percent of Christians.

When we depend on an "evangelism tool" or the "Five Easy Steps" to bring about new life, we are expecting the tool or resource to produce the result. We are trying to *produce* new life rather than *reproduce* new life. Reproduction requires the DNA of the gospel to be communicated in the context of relationship in order for new birth to occur. I'm not denigrating the usefulness of the evangelistic tool, but if I give you this tool and say, "If you'll just use this, people will come to know Jesus," am I not putting my trust in the tool? It's the *process* of reproduction that we've described up until now, culminating in relationship, that allows reproduction. The tool does not cause reproduction. Do you see the difference? There must be intimacy.

The Proper Environment

Next there must be the right environment for fertilization and impregnation. The environment has two elements that work in tandem. The first element is the condition of a man's heart, or his openness to receive the gospel. The second element is the completing work of the Holy Spirit. These principles are illustrated in the parable of the sower, found in Matthew 13:1–23, Mark 4:1–20 and Luke 8:4–15. In each of these passages, the environment of the heart determines the effectiveness of the gospel in the "soil" of a person's life. If the environment is fertile, new life will begin and the cycle continues. If the environment is hostile, the possibility of new life is either greatly diminished or missing. When new birth does occur, the pursuit of God has begun. The spiritual baby must then be nourished on the Word and brought to maturity in Christ alongside fellow believers. Notice that *the process is not complete until the offspring is reproducing.*

The Elements of Spiritual Reproduction

I must have **God's DNA**.

I must be a **willing and able instrument**.

Reproducing new birth **requires intimacy**.

There must be the **right environment for fertilization**.

There must be **impregnation**.

There must be **spiritual birth** through the Holy Spirit.

The process requires **nurturing towards maturity**.

The cycle is completed when the **offspring is reproducing**.

Birthing Is Not Reproduction

Many times we confuse *the event of spiritual birth* with *the process of reproduction*. We mistakenly feel that birth completes the process. In the church, evangelism or new birth, is often the whole focus at the expense of reproduction. The complete process involves all of the elements of spiritual reproduction. The Great Commission is a call to reproduce.

Reproductive Language

That night at the men's conference, after hearing the teaching from Joshua about circumcision, I went back and began to read the language of the gospel in the New Testament. I came to John 3 where Jesus uses the example of physical reproduction to describe the spiritual birth process. It's obvious that Nicodemus perceives this parallel when he says, in verse 4, "How can a man be born when he is old? Surely he cannot enter a second time into his mother's womb to be born!" He's not mistaking the language. Christ is using figurative language in communicating with Nicodemus, drawing a parallel between physical and spiritual birth. Do you see that the gospel is pictured as spiritual reproduction? If we're going to carry out the gospel, we must participate in spiritual reproduction.

It's obvious from every quantitative measure that the church is not reproducing. We must establish a pathway to reproduce spiritual fathers if we're going to change this trend. But the enemy has found that the easiest way to interrupt this process is to stop reproduction. Do you see the progression and why the building of spiritual fathers is so important? Without the pathway, we can identify the problem, we can see the needs; but unless we are building spiritual fathers we are going to continue to see the decline of the church.

Church Leadership Growth Path

Have you experienced a pathway in the church that is designed to move a man from spiritual immaturity to spiritual maturity—from spiritual childhood to spiritual fatherhood? Most of us have not. How can we develop that path and what should it look like?

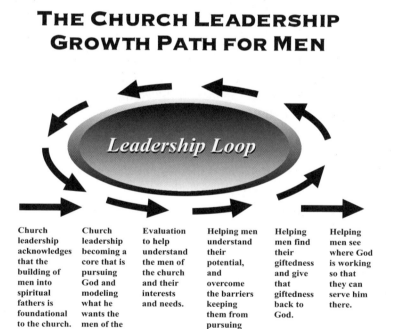

THE CHURCH LEADERSHIP GROWTH PATH FOR MEN

Leadership Loop

| Church leadership acknowledges that the building of men into spiritual fathers is foundational to the church. | Church leadership becoming a core that is pursuing God and modeling what he wants the men of the church to become. | Evaluation to help understand the men of the church and their interests and needs. | Helping men understand their potential, and overcome the barriers keeping them from pursuing God. | Helping men find their giftedness and give that giftedness back to God. | Helping men see where God is working so that they can serve him there. |

Here you can see a graphic representation of this growth path with a progressive process at the bottom of the diagram going from left to right.

The first column illustrates the importance of the affirmation that the building of men into biblical, godly leaders is foundational to the church. The second column states there must be a core of male leaders living out the pursuit of God so that they can lead the rest of the men of the church into that pursuit. The third column indicates that we must know who the men of our church are and where they are in regard to their interests and needs. The fourth column communicates the importance of challenging men to accept their calling to influence others and to see the positive potential impact they can have. The fifth column conveys the significance of helping men see their giftedness and understand the importance of giving their gifts back to God. In the last column we see that it is crucial to find where God is working and join him there.

Above the church pathway in the diagram is the "Leadership Loop," illustrating the reproductive cycle that must accompany the pathway. The terms "Leadership Loop" and "reproduction" are virtually synonymous. A leadership core is essential, but if these leaders don't reproduce themselves in future generations of leaders, they will wear out, and leadership in the church will become extinct. The leadership core must be willing to be the firstfruits, the DNA of leadership that multiplies in the rest of the men in the church. Do you agree this is imperative for the church?

What Needs to Happen?

- There needs to be a consensus that the building of men into mature leaders is foundational to the church.
- We need to identify leaders who are willing to pioneer the process. It will require their pastors, including the senior pastor, participating and reproducing with these pioneers who are becoming what they want their men to become.
- These pioneers must watch for, and identify, the plan that God is revealing to them. At some point, they must invite the rest of the men of the church to taste what they are experiencing and join them in the process.
- They must be continually asking the question: *What is keeping our men from pursuing God?* The answers to this question will help them remove the barriers that keep men from pursuing God.

Involvement of Church Leadership

Without leadership committed to and involved in the process of building men, the church will suffer and ministry to men will be perceived as a program focused on "good principles." But this program will fail! It is critically important for each generation of leaders to go through the same process of growth so that they share the same vision and move in unity in the same direction. Every church needs all of its leaders to understand how imperative their role is in reproducing leaders who become spiritual fathers.

Offering More to Men

Currently in the church, we are challenging men to be godly men, good husbands, and good fathers. But inwardly, men are shaking their heads and saying, "Who is a model of this in my church? How can I get there? Where is the pathway?" The typical church has no pathway to help men get there. Without a pathway, men are desperate and inwardly dying as they search for significance while lacking a place to become spiritual fathers who do spiritual fathering.

I recently heard George Barna state that in America there are twenty million "de-churched" adults—those who were once in the church and have now left. It's apparent that men, young and old, are saying, "I want to grow closer to God with other men in the church, but how do I do this?" Barna's statistic is pointing to the magnitude of the crisis in the church. Many men are walking away disappointed and disenchanted with the depth of relationships they are finding in the church.

Skipping the Foundational Steps

I believe that the majority of ministry to men in the church is ineffective. It has bypassed the initial foundational steps illustrated in the growth path diagram and is solely focused on the fourth element: *reestablishing the value of men.* In the typical church, men's ministry is focused on programs that center on felt needs while attempting to establish or build "better" men. This focus is largely unproductive. There must be a foundational leadership core that is modeling and reproducing a passion for God through a life process. If we only focus on the fourth element of the pathway, then the ministry will become all about a man's needs and not about the goal of spiritual reproduction.

A Man's Giftedness

The natural next step after calling men to their potential impact is to help men understand their giftedness. Many churches try to do this through specific programs. They focus on a man's giftedness to *do* good works rather than to *become* reproducing spiritual fathers. How can we speak of "giftedness" without sharing the incredible picture that every man is given the power by God to become a spiritual father building into the lives of others? Can we afford to overlook this any longer?

What Is the Process of Building a Pathway?

We've just finished an overview of the principles of the growth path diagram, and now we want to look at it again—focusing on the practical application of the principles for building a pathway. In the pages of this book we cannot give you an exact pathway to copy, but we can help you identify the general elements essential for your church's unique pathway. The value is in *experiencing* the reproductive dynamic of God building *his pathway* within your church. This pathway needs to be built from what God is speaking to you rather than having someone else determine what your pathway should be.

Pathway Building Blocks

The understanding and commitment of the leadership to building men determines the spiritual life and health of the church. *The first building block is for the senior pastor, and the functional leaders of the church, to affirm that the building of men into godly, mature, spiritual fathers is foundational to the church.* It is essential that they not just approve of the concept, but *become an integral part of the process.* For men to come together and build a pathway, without the heart and passion of the senior pastor and leaders, is difficult at best. Many times this leads to divisiveness in the church. It is best to pray and encourage the leaders, waiting until they are ready to join in and lead the process.

When the leadership understands the importance of building men, it is then time to focus on the second building block of the process: *A leadership core must begin to experience together what they want the rest of the men to experience.* This process of the core discovering and modeling the pathway to build men is missing in most churches. There are a number of barriers that keep men from pursuing God, and these need to be addressed by the leadership core and overcome. The ultimate goal is to reproduce the passionate pursuit of God in the men of the church. Therefore, these leaders must process through the barriers and affirm the calling to all the men of the church to become spiritual fathers.

The third building block is to seek out the needs, desires, and condition of the men of the church. We must survey and listen to the men of the church so that we can meet them where they are and lead them to where they need to be.

The fourth building block of the church is to introduce men to the potential that they have to influence and build others. Much of what has been traditional men's ministry has focused on reestablishing the positive image of a man. But if the foundational building blocks for the pathway are missing, the men cannot mature and reach their destiny. It is at this step that each new generation of leaders must be identified and taken through the same process that the core group went through, insuring that each generation of leaders will be unified with the same vision and mission.

The intent of the fifth building block is to help each man understand the gifts that he possesses—spiritually, physically, intellectually, vocationally, etc.—and that he should offer them back to God. It is important to understand that God's covenant to us as sons is all-sufficient, and our actions can earn us nothing. To this great gift of grace there is only one reasonable and appropriate response: to offer our personal gifts back to God.

In the last building block we are ready to see that God is offering us the opportunity to participate with him in the very act of spiritual reproduction. We must stay focused on and in relationship with God to see where he is working and join him there. It is in this process that we become spiritual fathers. God does not use perfect men; he uses men who are committed to the process of "becoming."

Reproduction Versus Production

What is the difference between *reproduction* and *production?* Reproduction is about becoming and production is about knowledge—knowing *about* something or someone. Reproduction is about relationships and production is about programs. Reproduction is about multiplication and production is about addition. Reproduction is about transformation and production is about reformation. Which lifestyle or focus do you want to represent your life and ministry?

Reproduction Versus Production

Becoming	Knowing about
Relationships	Programs
Multiplication	Addition
Transformation	Reformation

Without reproduction all we get is transfer growth. *Without reproduction we participate in managing the disintegration of the church.* All we will do is attempt to attract a larger percentage of a smaller pool of Christians to our churches.

Igniting the Pathway

The pathway, or reproductive place in the church, can't happen here today as you read this. But understanding reproduction can be an igniting point, allowing God to give you a vision and commitment for the process. It will be messy, it will take time, and it will require commitment, but it could be one of the most important decisions you will ever make. If your goal is instant impact or change, a reproductive pathway will not provide it. If your goal is transformation, then this is the way to experience it.

We must put into place a pathway where leaders, men who are involved in the passionate pursuit of God, can prepare to reproduce their heart and passion in the rest of the men of the church. The pathway must be visible, joinable, definable, and populated by the leaders in the church—a place where servant leaders are on the pathway saying, "Come and join us as we struggle through the messiness of life." These leaders must have a clear vision to pass on God's DNA to others so that each man has the opportunity to "become" a spiritual father.

A reproductive pathway will always be multigenerational—that is, men reproducing generations of spiritual fathers who pursue God and reproduce that pursuit in others. It should be the normative way in the church for men to move toward maturity and spiritual fatherhood. The hope is that every man in the church would be somewhere on the pathway and would be inviting other men who should be on the pathway to join him.

Let me end this chapter with a picture of how this takes place in the lives of men.

Spiritual Grandchildren

It was fourteen years ago that Jim and Mark connected through a church ministry in Ottumwa, Iowa. "I immediately picked up that this was an extremely difficult time in Mark's life," said Jim. "I could tell Mark needed me to help him focus on 'being' a godly man before spending significant time on 'doing' for God."

Jim made the strong commitment to meet with Mark once a week and become a spiritual mentor in his life. Their relationship continued to deepen and grow as the years went by. Jim said, "Mark needed somebody to watch his back in the battles of life." They became involved as Key Man/Ambassadors with Promise Keepers, and during this time Jim saw how vital their time together had been. He said, "God used me to help set Mark free. I could see that he had huge plans for Mark's life."

As Mark and Jim were introduced to Building Brothers, the year-long Building Brothers process seemed to give Mark the vehicle to deeply build into the lives of men with. During this time, Mark was introduced to Brian or "Bubba" as his friends call him. In their weekly Building Brothers group, Mark started developing a relationship with Bubba and dug deep into Bubba's life. "Bubba had a lot of deep wounds, but God used Mark to help heal them; Bubba quickly became a maturing believer with a heart to serve God," said Jim. Mark has gone on to take a group of struggling, young men through the year-long Building Brothers process. He has a deep commitment and desire to mentor others. In fact, Bubba has become one of the key leaders in the church with his skills to continue this process forward in the years to come.

Jim shared, "I clearly see that my job is not the 'out-front' leader, but rather one whose prime function is to mentor the leaders of tomorrow. God continues to lead me to those types of men, helping them become everything they are intended to be, going beyond my abilities and reproducing themselves."

Opportunity or Obligation

We've established the importance of reproduction, but the question that remains is *What will we reproduce?* It is the pursuit of God that must be reproduced. First John 2:12–14 clearly indicates that the DNA of reproduction is the pursuit of God. In the following section we will delve deeply into that pursuit. Do you see the living out of your relationship with God as an opportunity or an obligation?

Part IV

Pursuing God

Chapter 11

Is Your Relationship with God an Opportunity or Obligation?

Like the lost man, many men quickly fall into a common trap: we find it difficult to accept help. We get frantic in our efforts to find our way home out of the wilderness. It seems we, as men, feel that if we can put enough effort into the right formula we will earn the right to get what we want. When it comes to the Christian life, many of us are either trying to be "good enough" so that God will love us, or we are trying to find the "formula" to cause God to give us the life we want.

The Heart of the Message

We have previously looked at three of the four universal barriers that keep men from pursuing God: the father vacuum shapes the way we perceive God, the absence of a safe place in the church for men keeps men in a defensive posture, and the lack of trust—due to a lack of servant leadership—makes it difficult for us to follow or be followed into the process. The fourth barrier that will sidetrack a man's relationship with God is the trap of obligation.

There are two faces of obligation: trying to earn God's love, which leads to isolation, or trying to control God, which leads to bitterness. The first face demands that I do the right things and be good enough so that God will love me. But the question must be asked: *Can we ever be good enough to make God love us?* The second face implies that if I can discover the right pattern or formula, I can obligate God or manipulate him into doing what I want. It's important to ask: *Can we ever control God?*

In both strategies of relating to God we are working or struggling so hard that we've taken our eyes off of the cross of Christ. He was the only sacrifice and the only righteousness sufficient to provide us the freedom to approach the throne of God (Hebrews 10:19–23). In his letter to the Galatians, Paul clearly states that we may feel obligated to earn our way or become righteous, but that it is by grace, and grace alone, that we are made righteous. In Ephesians 2:8–9, Paul tells us: "For it is by grace you have been saved, through faith and this not from yourselves, it is the gift of God not by works, so that no one can boast."

We have been given the opportunity to know God, and through that relationship to have our deepest desires met. By knowing him, we can experience being loved by him. So how do we grasp this opportunity?

Going Deeper

Two Faces of Obligation

In the mid-1990s, I was traveling around the country training men who were going to teach others the principles of men's ministry. These men were some of the most committed in the nation, and they were there by invitation only. I started to ask them individually about their relationship with God, and the majority answered by describing their personal time with him in one of two ways. The first response went like this: "I haven't had my quiet time, so I can't approach God." The second response was similar: "If I don't have my quiet time, I will have a bad day."

Would either of these two statements describe your feelings about your quiet time and relationship with God? Let's look deeper at what they imply.

Obligation Is Legalism

"I haven't had my quiet time, so I can't approach God." This statement is similar in essence to the struggle with legalism that the apostle Paul was addressing in Galatians. Judaizers had infiltrated the churches in Galatia, teaching the Gentile converts that in order to be a Christian, belief in Christ as Savior was not enough—they also had to obey the law and be circumcised. Paul proclaimed, "It is for freedom that Christ has set us free. Stand firm, then, and do not let yourselves be burdened again by a yoke of slavery. Mark my words! I, Paul, tell you that if you let yourselves be circumcised, Christ will be of no value to you at all. Again I declare to every man who lets himself be circumcised that he is obligated to obey the whole law. You who are trying to be justified by law have been alienated from Christ; you have fallen away from grace" (Galatians 5:1–4).

As men of God, we seem to feel that if we follow a prescribed pattern of behavior, we can make ourselves more acceptable to God. Somehow I've got to clean myself up to the point where I'm good enough that God should love me. We feel that our right actions should make us worthy. Can we ever be "good enough" that God should love us? Paul clearly tells the Galatians and us that it is only by grace that we can be loved and accepted by God. When we add *anything* else, we put ourselves back under the law and we *obligate* ourselves to the law.

So, what is the result of approaching God from this standpoint? Doesn't this approach guarantee that we're going to stay estranged and isolated from him?

My Journey with Obligation

I would like to be able to tell you that I don't live in obligation, but when I look back at my life I find that at times I do. A number of years ago a friend approached me and asked if I would assist in saving a one-hour photo company that was in trouble. About six weeks into this huge undertaking it became apparent there were internal issues that were irresolvable, so the company began the process of shutting down. I was never paid for my time. I began to feel depressed and wasn't sure why I was having these feelings. I then realized I was listening to a subtle voice in my head saying, "You're inadequate because you haven't provided for your family." I worked but I didn't get paid. It didn't have anything to do with my performance, it wasn't my deficiency, but I was feeling defeated because I hadn't taken care of my obligation to support my family. Do you see what I was doing? I accepted the lie that I had to have a perfect result to be acceptable to God and my family. In like manner, don't we often think that we've got to live perfectly to be acceptable to God?

After an extended period of struggle, God revealed to me that I had the *opportunity* to know him through my relationship with him, but there was nothing I could do to make myself more acceptable to him. I finally felt free, and through that freedom, began to enter into a new dimension of relationship with Jesus as I walked with him throughout the day. But even though I continue to experience this freedom, there are still times when I struggle and feel unable to approach God.

What would you do if Billy Graham or someone of equal influence and stature in the Christian community called and asked for a little of your time on a regular basis, communicating that he felt that having a relationship with you would make him more effective in his ministry? "If you are willing," he says, "I will fly in to spend time with you." Would you take advantage of this opportunity to know him and be a part of his ministry? Would you make an effort to keep your schedule open so that you could do it?

The Creator God is offering a much greater opportunity to be with him. There is nothing that we must do to approach him. Will you take him up on the offer and accept his grace? Or will you hold back, feeling obligated to do the right things before you can approach him?

Freedom = **Grasping the Opportunity** *= Obedience*
or
Slavery = **Obligation** *= Legalism*

Punch Card Christianity

"If I don't have my quiet time, I will have a bad day." This is the second side of obligation, and it's even more insidious than the first. How many times have you heard a man say, "I had a great quiet time and so I'm going to have a great day?" What is he really saying? I did the right thing by getting my Christian punch card punched. What does this brand of Christianity do to us? Even if you're diligent and you have that card all punched up, are you always going to get what you want? This viewpoint assumes that by doing the right things we can somehow *obligate* God to keep us from pain and give us the life we want.

Aren't we also saying that if I do the right things and "follow the list," I can manipulate God? This list can be as simple as something I was taught as a child, something I've heard on Christian radio, or following the steps prescribed by the plethora of Christian self-help books. I say, "I can get anything I want because he owes me." Does God ever owe us anything?

I find that it is in times of personal crisis that the lie of obligation is revealed. This trap leads many of us into disappointment, disillusionment, anger, and bitterness—and ultimately leads to despair. If I have done all the right things it's easy to feel that, because I have completed the list, I am acceptable to God and he should then be *obligated* to keep me from pain and give me the life that I want. But what if things don't turn out as I expected? If I lose my job? If my marriage fails? If my child rebels? If I get cancer? If my wife or child gets cancer? Did I have the wrong list? Did I not know God? Or did I not understand the relationship that God offers me? What should my response be?

Have you ever felt this—that you had done the right thing and yet God hadn't delivered on his end of the bargain? What did that do to your relationship with God? Let me share my journey into these difficult waters.

Matthew's Story

Many years ago, I went through the pain of losing a son who was not quite two years old. Matthew was born in January of 1977. He was a happy, bright little boy. When he was about eighteen months old, I got a call from my wife, Jan, telling me that Matthew was in intensive care at the local hospital. I rushed down to the hospital and saw him in the children's ICU. The doctors thought he had contracted a virus of the heart and that things would be OK. They *weren't* OK.

Over the next six months, little Matthew got weaker and weaker. Even though we prayed diligently, called the elders and anointed him with oil, obtained the best medical resources, and believed that he would be healed, his condition did not improve. Sometime in the fall I began to realize that things couldn't go on the way they were, but I didn't even want to think about the alternative.

The day before Matthew died, I knew that he was going to die even though the doctors were telling Jan that we would have him until summer. I was alone at our house while Jan was at the hospital. I remember fighting and wrestling with God. I told him that he could not take my son. After about four hours, I came to a point where I said, "I can't do this. You are God, so you have to do it through me." I began to stop demanding and I said, "God, you need to empty me out so that I can do what you, and my family, need me to do in the next hours and days." I made preparations so Jan and I could stay at the hospital. But when I got there, she was so convinced he was going to live that I couldn't find it in me to make her stay. We went home and Matthew lived until the next morning, and then I watched my son die.

This was not the end of my struggle, but the beginning. The year following Matthew's death was one of the most difficult in my life. If you had asked me prior to this time to describe the relationship between God and his people, I would have given you all of the right answers. I would have told you that we are his servants and we are here to bring him glory. Even though that is what I would have told you, deep down inside I had bought into a gospel that said that if you do the right things, have a quiet time, tithe, attend church, and so on, God would keep you from suffering.

My real response was more like this: "What the hell are you doing, God? I have spent most of my life trying to serve you. Why in the world didn't you protect me?" That was what I was feeling at a gut level. Have you ever been there—the point where you say, "God, you were supposed to keep me from feeling pain?" This was a crisis point for me. Either I didn't know who God was or I didn't have the right relationship with him. I remember standing there wounded and abandoned, and the only thing that kept me moving toward God was that I told other men that he was "the answer." At this time, it was now almost impossible *not* to give him the opportunity to be *the* answer.

Over time, God confirmed the nature of our relationship. He had given me the *opportunity* to know him and to be part of what he was doing. Through that I could find tremendous significance, but there was no way that *I* could guarantee that I would not feel pain or be more acceptable to God. I was given the opportunity to know him when I became his son, but my own actions would *never* obligate him to keep me safe nor give me what I wanted.

True Obedience

What will *you* choose: opportunity or obligation? Your choice will determine whether you live a life characterized by gratitude and joy or by bitterness and isolation. I want to challenge you to grasp the opportunity to live in freedom by being obedient to God. In your mind right now, you may be saying, "I understand the concept of choosing the opportunity to know God, but what does that look like in real life? How do I get from where I am now to where I am grasping the opportunity to live in obedience to God?"

The day you received Christ Jesus as your Lord and Savior you began the process of desiring true obedience. From there, the Holy Spirit gave you a new heart attitude to know God and to please him. Romans 6:22 says, "Now that you have been set free from sin and have become slaves to God, the benefit you reap leads to holiness, and the result is eternal life."

Paul's letter to the Galatians forces us to ask the question, "What am I a slave to?" Is it sin, legalism, or Christ? We must choose the opportunity of obedience over legalism and understand that this is the harder of the two roads and the path less chosen by many in the Christian community.

True obedience is doing the right thing, for the right reasons, in the right way, at the right time. I want you to read that again. If any one of the pieces is missing, it's not obedience.

An example of this is illustrated in 2 Samuel 6 when David decided the ark of the covenant needed to be brought to Jerusalem. Was that the right thing to do? Yes, it was. Did he want it to be there for the right reason? I believe so. Now we come to the important issue: When David went down to get it, what did he do? He allowed it to be transported on a cart, which wasn't God's way. Do you remember what happened? When the ark got jostled, a man named Uzzah reached out to steady it— and God struck him dead.

It says in the passage that David was angry and fearful, probably the same feelings I felt that day when Matthew was dying. But we know from the parallel passage in 1 Chronicles 15 that David chose the right response in seeking the heart of God. He read the Law of Moses and found that the ark was to be carried by the Levites, with poles on their shoulders. As the ark was transported to Jerusalem in the Lord's pre-scribed manner, David was so excited that he danced in a way that offended his wife, Saul's daughter, Michal.

Do you see the issue? Earlier, David was doing the right thing and he was doing it for the right reason, but he was not doing it in the right way. Obedience is not choosing a shortcut or the easy way out! When we fully obey, we are afforded the opportunity to know Christ intimately. We are fools if we don't grasp the opportunity to know Christ.

True Obedience

- Doing the right thing
- For the right reasons
- In the right way
- At the right time

*Obedience is not choosing
the easy way out.*

Choosing to Live in Freedom

I believe that the very nature of our relationship with God will be determined by how we choose to live. We can be caught up in obliga-tion—either trying to earn our way to God or trying to discover the formula to manipulate him. If we do that, we're going to be isolated from God because we're never good enough or we're going to be embittered with God because he didn't keep his end of the bargain. Or, we can choose the opportunity to be in relationship with the Living God.

In this battle between opportunity and obligation we live in tension as followers of Christ. How do I grasp the opportunity to communicate with God? How do I grasp the opportunity to work through conflict and wrestle with him, like I did that day over Matthew? How do I grasp the opportunity to be in covenant with him, where I realize what he's promised to me and what my reasonable response should be to those promises? How do I grasp the opportunity to co-labor with him? You see, each time I am brought back to the watershed issue, which is the choice between opportunity and obligation.

I can say, "What is the program? Show me the list. Give me the legalistic formula so I can prove I'm all right." Or I can grasp the opportunity that Jesus' blood has provided me. It is through the cross that I engage him. And it is through the intimacy of my relationship with him that I am able to be a reproducer with his DNA and become a spiritual father.

In the next five chapters we will journey through this progression.

Chapter 12

Are You Committed to the Battle?

The lost man had clearly lost sight of his goal. Was it to find his way back to camp, or to shoot an elk even though he had no idea where he was? The man who was lost couldn't move with confidence in any direction until he could affirm the goal and commit to it. Many men have this same struggle with committing to life in the church because they are not being called to a clear mission or goal. Are Christian men called to perfection, or is the mission to be committed to the process of becoming a spiritual father?

The Heart of the Message

If we enter into the Christian life by grace, why do most of us feel that our works are necessary to sanctify or perfect us? We are caught in this dilemma. If we accept the notion that perfection is the standard, and yet know that we are flawed; how can we ever meet the standard? The harder we work at being perfect, the farther we seem to fall from the goal.

The apostle Paul faced this same dilemma. In 1 Corinthians 15:9 he says, "For I am the least of the apostles and do not even deserve to be called an apostle." He continues in 1 Timothy 1:15, "Christ Jesus came into the world to save sinners—of whom I am the worst." We can clearly see that the more Paul matures in the Christian life, the more he experiences his human sinfulness. So, achieving perfection by our own efforts is certainly not a viable goal. What is the answer, then?

Could it be that our sanctification can only be acquired by God's grace and not by our works? In 2 Timothy 4:7 Paul says, "I have fought the good fight, I have finished the race, I have kept the faith." He clearly indicates that our part in sanctification is to commit to the battle and not turn back; but it is by God's grace alone that righteousness is given to us through Christ Jesus. So, we are not found righteous because of our own efforts, but by trusting in God and continuing to experience the fullness of his grace.

Going Deeper

Growth in Theory

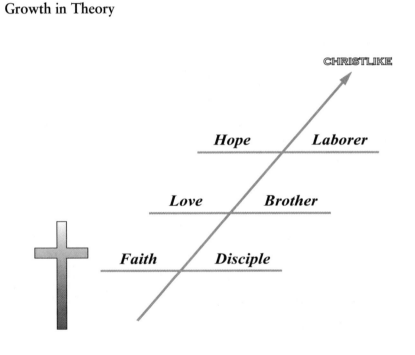

The "Growth in Theory" diagram is a typical drawing used to help describe the Christian life in understandable steps. We've been told, and it's been presented as the model, to expect the Christian life to be as neat and clean as this diagram. We enter in by faith at the cross as a disciple, we become brothers through love, and we end up experiencing hope, which leads us to becoming a laborer in the kingdom. Does your life look as "clean" and step-oriented as this straight line? Or is your experience of the Christian life more like the next diagram?

Growth in Reality

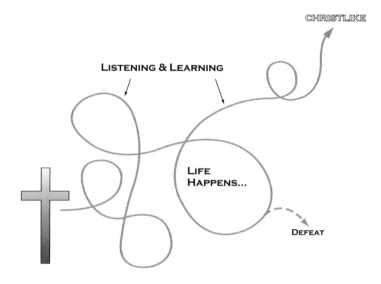

This is more like it, isn't it? Our lives are a series of ups and downs—momentary victories and momentary failures. When we stay in the process, focusing on God, he is able to use all of those experiences to shape us into the image of his Son. It is not by having a neat, perfect life that we are able to serve God and be used by him, but rather, by remaining committed to him through all of the circumstances of life.

What is Victorious Christian Living?

Victorious Christian living is not perfection. It is not following the prescribed faultless life pattern. *Victorious Christian living is entering into the battle and never turning back.* It's important to understand that God has called us to be committed to him. All we have to do is hang on to him and stay in the process. Without that commitment we're not going to persevere and experience the blessing of the victorious Christian life.

We're going to be perfected by being in God's presence when we stand before him at the resurrection (1 John 3:2), but we're not going to be perfected now. We're in the process of being perfected, and that's the key. If we call men to, and demand the end result of perfection, we are guaranteeing their failure. But if we call them to the process, they will not fail.

Many of us as men and leaders feel we're not fully acceptable to God until we're perfect. What does accepting the obligation of perfection do to us? It shuts us down. We are defeated before we even start. When I'm personally challenged to be a godly man and misunderstand this challenge to be a call to perfection, I am caught in the trap of obligation. I can't get there from here. It's like saying, "Dan, I want you to go out in the parking lot and fly." There actually is a way for me to fly. If you give me the right equipment and training, then I could go out and fly. But for you to challenge me to fly without the support and process to accomplish it, guarantees my failure! If we continue to define victorious Christian living as perfection, we are doing the same thing to our men.

Giving Freedom Through Transparency

Part of the problem is how we as leaders present the Christian life. Our struggles and moments of failure are rarely exposed or shared. Instead, we typically present the Christian life like this: "My wife and I are serving the Lord, I led seventeen people to Christ last week, I teach three Bible studies, and my children are all on the mission field." This picture of life leaves people saying, "I barely got out of bed this morning!" You and I need to be men who other men can identify with—leaders who expose their struggles and model the process of sanctification for men to follow. The man who reveals his struggles with God is a person other men can identify with and follow.

I remember a time early in the movement of Promise Keepers when a well-known speaker stood up and shared his struggle with masturbation. (It was at that point that I knew this wasn't my mother's church.) You could have heard a pin drop, even though five thousand men were present. I'll bet the bulk of those men almost fell out of their chairs because they had never heard this talked about in their church. Although I'm sure it was uncomfortable, I know they also must have felt a deep sense of freedom because of this speaker's honesty about this sensitive subject.

A Roaring Lion

The nature of the Christian life is battle. Let's look at some of the images of battle that Peter shared in 1 Peter 5:8–9. "Be self-controlled and alert. Your enemy the devil prowls around like a roaring lion looking for someone to devour. Resist him, standing firm in the faith, because you know that your brothers throughout the world are undergoing the same kind of sufferings." Do you hear the battle terms that are used? Why should we be alert? Because we are in a common battle and our brothers throughout the world are experiencing the same thing. Every one of us is in it. When we present the Christian life as a clean, straight, and sterile line, we've just castrated and isolated the men in our church.

Peter Hathaway Capstick, a professional big-game hunter, writes about one of his experiences with lions in his book *Death in the Long Grass*. He recounts a time when he was sent in to kill a lion that had eaten an African woman. He was experienced enough to realize the importance of choosing a good tracker to hunt this lion down. He and the tracker find themselves going down a bloody trail where they spot a hand that's been bitten off lying in the dirt. What would you do? Run?

Capstick begins to think about lion attacks that he has experienced in the past. Here in the bush country a lion usually attacks from less than forty yards. We think a wide receiver is quick if he can run forty yards in four seconds. A lion can cover one hundred yards in four seconds. But a charging lion is not coming from one hundred yards. Its charge will cover only twenty to forty yards. This means that, from the time he comes at you to the time he reaches you, you have only one or two seconds to respond. Capstick writes that a lion will show just a little bit of movement, or sometimes he'll even roar before he attacks, to focus your attention and make you hesitate. The apostle Peter illustrates this strategy in 1 Peter 5:8. This roar is intended to momentarily paralyze the prey. When the lion roars, it takes away the second we have to react. He's won!

The hunters move farther along the trail and all of a sudden Capstick hears a sound and the lion is on him. He doesn't even have time to get the barrels of the gun turned around. The gun goes off as the lion comes over the top of him. He's spinning around and reaching for the gun, but he can't find it. He hears a holler off to his right—it's his tracker. The tracker could have said, "Let me get my tail out of here." He doesn't do that. He calls the lion to him. The tracker's spear does nothing to slow down the lion and instantly it's on top of him, chewing on his arm.

Capstick is now in the position that his tracker had been in. He could have said, "He's bit the dust. He's probably dead, anyway, so I'm going to save myself!" He doesn't do that. He moves toward the ongoing battle and quickly tries to find the gun, but the only thing he can get his hand on is the broken half of the spear. He rams it into the top of the lion's neck and kills the beast.[i]

A Deep Bond

So why am I telling you this? I want you to see the importance of staying in the battle. You've got two men from different racial backgrounds. They are from different cultures, but they've developed a relationship and their very lives depend upon one another. Because of their commitment to each other, neither one of them is willing to leave the fray. The fact is that at the end of the day they are only alive because of this.

This is the picture given to us in 1 Peter 5:8–9. In the tremendous rush of the attack, when our very survival depends upon each man's commitment and response, we need brother warriors who will come to our aid—or we will not survive. We are unable to develop these relationships of trust when we are under the lion's attack. We must develop these relationships *before* the attack. Do you see how important this is? We've got to grasp the opportunity to live in relationship and fight the common battle.

Enter the Battle and Don't Turn Back

What does the New Testament indicate will disqualify us from the spiritual battle? Jesus said, "No one who puts his hand to the plow and looks back is fit for service in the kingdom of God" (Luke 9:62). He is saying that the only way you can fail is to opt out of the process.

It's important to understand that if you stay in the battle, you will be bloodied. I've been involved in ministry to men since 1972, but in 1990, as God was birthing Promise Keepers, the spiritual battle in my life went off the charts and has remained there ever since. It didn't just increase; it exploded exponentially! I probably have been bloodied more in these last fifteen years than I was in the forty years before that. Are you experiencing the intensity of the battle? When you step into this process and begin to address the issue of building men into spiritual fathers, you are going to step into the heat of battle. Yet, I believe this battle is the very thing you desire and God made you for. As a man, you were made to be a warrior; and if you want to truly live, you better get into the battle. If you're not in the battle, you will die a slow and meaningless death inside.

Men must understand, and we as leaders must model for them, that victory is committing to the battle and never turning back.

God Uses Battle-scarred Veterans
The apostle Paul was wounded and bloodied throughout his entire ministry for the Lord. In 2 Corinthians 11:24–28 he wrote:

> Five times I received from the Jews the forty lashes minus one. Three times I was beaten with rods, once I was stoned, three times I was shipwrecked, I spent a night and a day in the open sea, I have been constantly on the move. I have been in danger from rivers, in danger from bandits, in danger from my own countrymen, in danger from Gentiles; in danger in the city, in danger in the country, in danger at sea; and in danger from false brothers. I have labored and toiled and have often gone without sleep; I have known hunger and thirst and have often gone without food; I have been cold and naked. Besides everything else, I face daily the pressure of my concern for all the churches.

If you're not willing to get bloodied, God can't fully use you. I want to be significantly used by him. Is that your desire? I don't like being bloodied, but it's inevitable in the Christian life. If we expect the

Christian life not to wound us, then we've limited how much God can use us. My challenge to you, putting it in a very masculine way, would be, "Do you have the testosterone to get into the battle even though you know you're going to be wounded?" If so, then I want to join with you. But if you accept the lie that the Christian life will not wound us, we can't battle together. The common battle is why we need each other. God made us to be warriors, and we've allowed Satan and the world to take that away from us.

Within the church, we've made many men timid or "nice." I'm sick and tired of "nice" Christian men. We present Christian manhood in the model of a soft, almost feminine male, and not in the model of William Wallace. You can define gentleness as strength and timidness as weakness. A man could not have lived through what Paul lived through and been timid. It takes battle-scarred veterans, like Paul, to fight the battle and to be able to carry the wounded off the battlefield.

If we're not willing to expose our scars, then we can't help the wounded. I need to be able to communicate to the man who is broken and on the ground bleeding, "See this scar? I've been exactly where you are and God healed me. He can heal you too." That type of battlefield commitment gives a man hope. Men need to hear from their leaders, "If you're wounded, I will come and get you. I'm not going to leave you." As leaders, we should respond like Lt. Col. Hal Moore in *We Were Soldiers*—being the first on the battlefield and the last to leave.

Are You Defeated in the Battle?

Freedom is found in living in the battle. The goal is the pursuit of God. *The goal isn't the destination; it's the journey.* Our part is to stay in the process—no matter how messy it gets—and never give up. Refer back to the arrow pointing to defeat in the "Growth in Reality" diagram illustrated earlier in this chapter. The arrow illustrates the crucial principle in the process: the only way you and I can fail is to opt out. Momentary failure doesn't mean that I have failed in the Christian life; it only means that I'm struggling. If I remain committed to the process, I am victorious.

Have you been feeling defeated because you haven't lived up to the standard of perfection? Does your life look more like the journey portrayed in the "Growth in Reality" diagram? If so, it is time to recommit to the battle and experience the freedom that can only come from living by faith and trusting God to complete the work that he has started in you (Philippians 1:6). If you have been on the sidelines feeling disqualified, I want to challenge you to grab hold of the plow and not look back. Enter into the battle and realize that God is not asking for perfection. He is asking for commitment.

Now that we have defined the nature of victorious Christian living, it is time to look at the elements of our relationship with Christ. We have just reinforced the importance of commitment, and now it's time to understand communication with Christ.

1 Peter Hathaway Capstick, Death in the Long Grass (New York: St. Martin's Press, 1977), 42-44

Chapter 13

How Do You Communicate With God?

The man lost in the woods initiated contact with me and then tried to communicate with me about his predicament, even though he wasn't fully able to trust me to help him become "found." Likewise, many Christian men struggle with approaching God and maintaining communication with him so that they can go from being "lost" to being "found." Living in relationship with God begins with communicating with God—speaking to him and listening to him.

The Heart of the Message

I had just come home from a long trip in Europe where it had been difficult to communicate with my family due to the time difference and my schedule. I was looking forward to being with them, so when I walked through the door we immediately sat down and began to reconnect: I was anxious to find out what had taken place in their lives while I was gone, as well as to tell them what God had been doing on my trip.

As I think back on that day I am struck by how differently we respond to God when we have been out of communication with him. We tend to pull away from him even farther, and consequently, feel that we have to do something or earn the right to reengage him. Why do we respond this way?

Do you remember the parable of the prodigal son in Luke 15? The younger son decided to take his inheritance and leave his family to go off into the world and make his own decisions. His plan worked just fine until hard times came; yet, he did not return home, most likely because he felt he had forfeited his rights as a son. When the prodigal became totally destitute and finally "came to his senses," he decided to return to his father and ask for forgiveness, even if he would only be treated as a servant. But the father, who had been waiting expectantly for him all along, ran out to meet him. He was eager for his son's return and for their relationship to be restored. The son's position had never changed in his father's eyes—even though he had stayed away, laboring under a lie. He only experienced the depth of his father's love and compassion when he was back home with him.

Is it possible that our enemy knows that if he can keep us estranged from God he can starve our relationship with God and keep us from maturing into the men we should be? If continual communication is the bedrock of a relationship, then it makes sense that if I'm stopped from communicating with God I will be kept from fully knowing Christ.

When my children were younger and acted disobediently, they responded to me in one of two ways: they either ran away to hide, or they came and hugged my legs. I tend to respond to God by running away when the circumstances of life or my lack of diligence keep me from communicating with him. How do you respond?

Going Deeper

What Does it Mean to Pursue God?

About ten years ago, a team of men and I started the initial process of trying to communicate the principle of "pursuing God." One of the major difficulties we faced while writing on this topic was the common terms we tend to use when describing the spiritual disciplines—terms such as "daily quiet time." Why do you think this was so difficult? Because the language we use in the church is inherently "obligation" language. We would write about "being in the Word," about prayer, etc., and there was "obligation" in everything we wrote. We finally began to understand that we couldn't communicate what God had put on our hearts if we used this language. If we were going to communicate effectively we had to begin to speak about our relationship with God in a different way.

We saw that God was calling us to a passionate relationship with him. It wasn't about a list of disciplines that must be followed to know him. We needed to use relational terms to effectively communicate. The question we needed to answer was, *What are the key elements of any healthy relationship?*

Elements of a Healthy Relationship

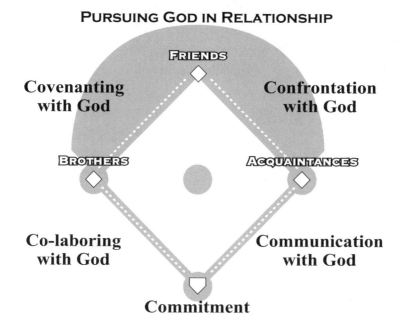

PURSUING GOD IN RELATIONSHIP

FRIENDS

Covenanting with God

Confrontation with God

BROTHERS

ACQUAINTANCES

Co-laboring with God

Communication with God

Commitment

The diagram above illustrates what I believe are the five elements in any healthy relationship. These elements are necessary whether we are talking about a relationship with God or with another person. In our relationship with God, the process starts with a level of commitment to him and moves into communication, confrontation, covenanting, and co-laboring. Let me briefly summarize these five elements before taking a deeper look at each of them in the rest of this chapter and in the next three chapters.

Commitment to God

How can you have a relationship if there's no commitment? You can have an "accommodation," but not a relationship. Whether in marriage, business, or the church, there must be commitment to work toward a healthy relationship.

Having a commitment to God starts with a choice but is sustained by continuing to grasp the opportunity to pursue him. Have you accepted Jesus Christ as Savior and Lord? Salvation is only the beginning of the process that threads throughout our entire lives. If you are God's son, then it's time to grasp the *opportunity* to pursue him in relationship. Are you continuing to choose to follow Jesus? Matthew 4:19–20 recounts the calling of Christ's first followers, "'Come, follow me,' Jesus said, 'and I will make you fishers of men.' At once they left their nets and followed him."

Communication with God

Communication with God is the second key element in having a relationship with God and pursuing him. I cannot think of any relationship in my life that will exist for very long without good, effective communication. In our relationship with God, it is the Word, worship, meditation, and prayer that allow us to communicate with him. Are you grasping the opportunity to walk in his presence?

Confrontation with God

Let's refer back to a statement we made previously in this book: *The depth of our relationships, whether with God or with others, will be determined by the level of conflict we are willing to journey through.* The commitment to journey through conflict with God is the third important element of our relationship with him. I want to suggest to you that you won't have a growing, healthy relationship unless you work through conflict. An unwillingness or avoidance to work through conflict limits, or even stops, the process of going deeper into relationship.

Covenanting with God

The fourth element is covenanting with God. Ongoing relationship depends on some kind of agreement or covenant determining how we are going to interact with one another. We usually informally work through the process of relationship without realizing we are building trust or a covenant with each other. We covenant with each other that, "If you respond a certain way, I'm going to respond back in a certain way." I believe every relationship at some level has a covenant. We need to be more aware of this in our relationship with God.

Co-laboring with God

There's a product that comes out of every relationship. The last element, co-laboring or co-creating with God, is the goal and result of a deepening relationship with Christ. Living at this co-laboring, co-creating level allows us to function as spiritual fathers.

I believe these five elements build upon one another, although they also operate simultaneously. In the rest of this chapter and in the next three chapters, we will dissect these elements and understand how they can revolutionize our relationship with God. A relationship with God can't happen through obligation! Having a relationship with God is not something I do to get something from God, but rather, it is grasping the opportunity to know and participate in what God is about.

The Relational Diamond

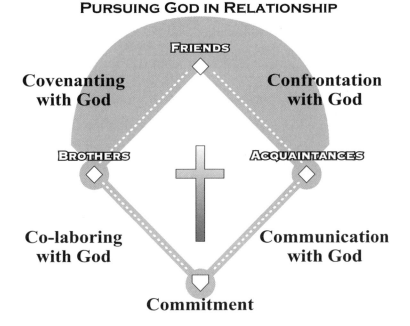

PURSUING GOD IN RELATIONSHIP

FRIENDS

Covenanting with God

Confrontation with God

BROTHERS

ACQUAINTANCES

Co-laboring with God

Communication with God

Commitment

It's important to tie this back into the "Relational Diamond" that we have shared throughout this book. These elements have the same impact whether they're with God or others. When I'm learning to communicate with God, I'm just beginning to get acquainted with him. Until I'm acquainted with him, I won't begin to experience his character and I'll never trust him in confrontation. But confrontation will allow me to become God's "friend" and lead me to covenanting with him. Covenanting with God will allow me to become his "brother," resulting in my co-laboring with him. Do you see how the levels build on each other and depend upon one another?

It's vital to realize that Christ is already here on this pathway in the Relational Diamond. That's why the image of the cross is in the center of the diamond. He doesn't need to develop a relationship with me; I need to *experience* a relationship with him. Do you see the difference? I must understand and accept that this is the way *I* pursue him while *he* pursues me.

Grasping the Opportunity to Communicate with God

If I don't have commitment, I can't proceed to the rest of the elements. Communication drives and supports my relationship all the way through the process and is essential to initiating and working through conflict. If the commonly understood principle that I need to pursue the opportunity of communication with my wife in order to have a healthy marriage relationship is true, is it not also true in my relationship with God? If I am living in obligation, I will try to earn the right to be in relationship with God. I will say, "I missed my quiet time, so I'm not worthy to approach you. Possibly, when I have earned the right, I'll communicate with you." What does that do to our relationship?

In contrast, our motivation toward God should be, "I've missed you, God, but I'm not going to miss the opportunity to communicate with you now." That is living in relationship. That is grasping the opportunity. I am not going to pull away from God; I am going to run to him.

The apostle Paul calls us to "be imitators of God ... as dearly loved children" (Ephesians 5:1). Think about that image for a moment. If you have ever been the father of a young child, what would happen when that child would see you coming? He or she runs and grabs one of those tree-trunk legs of yours. Does your son or daughter "imitate" your actions? That's the picture Paul gives us. Relationship is calling you and me to come and hug God's legs. It's only when we believe the lie of obligation that we disqualify ourselves. We don't feel worthy. We step back into the isolation. Do you see the obligation trap? And do you see the freedom that comes from understanding and grasping the opportunity to communicate with God?

Practicing the Presence of God

Brother Lawrence, in the seventeenth century, captured the lifestyle of communication, in his profound book, *The Practice of the Presence of God*. In the beginning of Brother Lawrence's journey toward God, his theology was pretty screwed up—he thought he would not be saved because he was clumsy and thus worthless to the kingdom. Even though his theology was defective, he began to pursue Christ and all of those misconceptions fell away.

He tells us: "I have not found my manner of life in books ... I have not followed all of these methods. On the contrary, although I do not know for what reason, I found they discouraged me ... I continued this way for some years, applying my mind carefully the rest of the day, and even in the midst of my business, to the presence of God, whom I considered always with me, and often as in me."[1]

Brother Lawrence learned to live in the presence of God. As soon as the communication was broken he quickly ran back to restore it. Because of that, he began to live in a whole new dimension that he had not known was possible.

I believe the same presence of God is available to each one of us. Will we run back and grab God's legs, or will we run away, hide, and try to earn our way back to him? Our negative response to God could actually be an offense to what Christ did for us on the cross. We say by our actions, "Your life given for me wasn't really enough. I must add something." Doesn't that communicate a level of arrogance? Am I not communicating that my actions are worth more than Christ's blood? This is a sobering thought.

Look at the opportunity we have: God is continually standing in front of us and not running away. In order to live in relationship with God, I've continually got to be grasping the opportunity to communicate with him. This is an opportunity you and I can't afford to miss.

Communicating with God

Let's dig deeper into the important element of communication with God. It has two major components—listening and speaking. We primarily hear from God through spending time in his Word, meditation, and quietness. We primarily speak to God through prayer and worship.

The heart attitude that allows us to hear God was modeled by Samuel in 1 Samuel 3:1–10:

> The boy Samuel ministered before the LORD under Eli. In those days the word of the LORD was rare; there were not many visions.
>
> One night Eli, whose eyes were becoming so weak that he could barely see, was lying down in his usual place. The lamp of God had not yet gone out, and Samuel was lying down in the temple of the LORD, where the ark of God was. Then the LORD called Samuel.
>
> Samuel answered, "Here I am." And he ran to Eli and said, "Here I am; you called me."
>
> But Eli said, "I did not call; go back and lie down." So he went and lay down.
>
> Again the LORD called, "Samuel!" And Samuel got up and went to Eli and said, "Here I am; you called me."
>
> "My son," Eli said, "I did not call; go back and lie down."
>
> Now Samuel did not yet know the LORD: The word of the LORD had not yet been revealed to him.
>
> The LORD called Samuel a third time, and Samuel got up and went to Eli and said, "Here I am; you called me."
>
> Then Eli realized that the LORD was calling the boy. So Eli told Samuel, "Go and lie down, and if he calls you, say, 'Speak, LORD, for your servant is listening.'" So Samuel went and lay down in his place.
>
> The LORD came and stood there, calling as at the other times, "Samuel! Samuel!"
>
> Then Samuel said, "Speak, for your servant is listening."

Attitudes and Actions of Communication

In this passage Samuel modeled three attitudes and actions that we must follow if we are to hear God: he was staying where God lived; there were no distractions to keep him from hearing; he was willing and ready to respond to what he heard. Are you, like Samuel, staying where God is? Are you in his Word so that you can hear him? Are you focused on him so that the distractions of life are not keeping you from hearing him? Are you willing and ready to respond to what you hear?

We can express our love and commitment through prayer and worship. These are complimentary parts of communicating with God. I often used the "ACTS" model of prayer to guide my interaction with God. I want to encourage you to use this as a general guide (not as a legalistic tool).

Adoration: affirming God's character and attributes

1. Who he is (e.g., his character, mercy, and love)
2. What he says (e.g., promises and truth)
3. What he does (e.g., righteous judgment and powerful deeds)

Confession: agreeing with God

1. In order to experience the forgiveness of sin. Read 1 John 1:7–10.
2. The continuing struggle with sin is evidence that we belong to God.
3. This is a time for honesty, not platitudes.
   Read Romans 7:14–25 to see this modeled.
   a. Honest struggle is the goal.
   b. Struggle is a mark of a man of God.
4. It keeps us focused on and experiencing grace.

Thanksgiving: for what he has done—even for those things that we do not understand, even when it is not easy. "Be joyful always; pray continually; give thanks in all circumstances, for this is God's will for you in Christ Jesus." (1 Thessalonians 5:16–18)

Supplication: sharing our desires and requests with God. "Do not be anxious about anything, but in everything, by prayer and petition, with thanksgiving, present your requests to God. And the peace of God, which transcends all understanding, will guard your hearts and your minds in Christ Jesus." (Philippians 4:6–7)

Worship as a Lifestyle

Worship is giving God worth, which includes the private and corporate expression of the first three elements of the ACTS model. Adoration, confession, thanksgiving, and *obedience* constitute a lifestyle of worship. This understanding of obedience as worship is based on Romans 12:1–2: "Therefore, I urge you, brothers, in view of God's mercy, to offer your bodies as living sacrifices, holy and pleasing to God—this is your *spiritual act of worship* (emphasis mine). Do not conform any longer to the pattern of this world, but be transformed by the renewing of your mind. Then you will be able to test and approve what God's will is—his good, pleasing and perfect will."

Most of us who are leaders have recognized that most men don't express worship in the church very well. It doesn't seem to matter what church, what denomination, or what style of worship we offer them. In my personal observation, I typically see about two out of ten men actually involve themselves in worship; the rest sit on their hands like the process is painful.

Part of the problem is that we have brought into the church the world's concept that our identity and self-esteem are built on our accomplishments. When we get into the presence of God and recognize his holiness, we begin to see the gulf between him and us. This contrast clearly points out how ugly and sinful we really are. We don't like this experience; it is not comfortable. Therefore, many of us avoid getting close enough to God to see our failure and respond to God's pattern of repentance. This tendency illustrates that our sense of self-esteem or worth is not built upon Christ's love, but rather on our performance.

It's important to understand why men don't worship well—in order to call them to a lifestyle of worship rather than to judge and isolate them. Too many men are deriving their identity and worth from the world rather than from their relationship with Christ. In response to this, we must take men back to worship as an essential element of their relationship with God so that they can experience the love of their heavenly Father who is saying, "I am pleased with you. I love you. I am safe."

If so many men are struggling with worship in a church service designed to encourage worship, how much more difficult is it for men to live a lifestyle of worship in every other area of their lives? Worship allows us to express our passion as men. It's imperative that we model a lifestyle of worship to men who are to become spiritual fathers.

Accepting the Gift of His Presence

If I have neglected the opportunity to commune with God, the Holy Spirit is quick to convict me of it. I must recognize it as sin, confess it, and ask forgiveness. Just as the father of the prodigal son welcomed him with open arms, our heavenly Father is ready to forgive us and welcome us back. Restoration is only a moment away if I will just turn to him rather than run away.

I really am a fool if I choose to miss these opportunities to pursue God. Unfortunately, this means I've been a fool quite a bit of my life. What about you? Are you being a wise man who will grasp the opportunity? Or are you being a fool—one who has the ability to step into and stay in the presence of the Living God but you're not doing it?

Will you grasp the opportunity that is yours as a child of God and continue to commune with him? It is this life of communication that gives us the confidence and the mechanism to journey through conflict with God. In the following chapter we will be looking at this foundational relational principle of growing through conflict.

1 Brother Lawrence, *The Practice of the Presence of God*, revised and rewritten by Harold J. Chadwick (North Brunswick, NJ: Bridge-Logos Publishers, 1999), 75.

Chapter 14

Should We Wrestle with God?

It was my willingness to confront the lost man by asking, "Who's lost—me or you?" that forced him to admit that he was lost and that he should listen to me. Without this confrontation he would have continued to be as lost as he was when he so frantically came out of the woods. We must live and work through confrontation to properly benefit from the relationships in our lives. Confrontation is the process that allows us to know where we are and where we need to be.

The Heart of the Message

Many of us desire a deeper relationship with God, but the pathway seems illusive. In fact, it's not only with God that we desire a deeper relationship, but also with our wives, children and friends. Why is it so difficult to go deeper?

In my life, I have found a universal principle to be true: the depth of our relationships will be determined by the level of conflict we are willing to work through. Conflict is inevitable in lasting relationships; therefore, for relationships to endure and grow, resolving conflict is imperative. Avoiding the opportunity to engage and wrestle through conflict with one another will only sentence us to weak, shallow relationships.

What about conflict with God? The principle that the depth of relationship will be determined by the level of conflict is particularly important in our relationship with God. Many of us would consider engagement with God at this level as forbidden or rebellious, so we avoid it. However, could our fear of being rebellious keep us from truly knowing God?

Over twenty-five years ago I was forced to face this very situation when my son Matthew died. I wrestled with God at a level in which I never had before. I shouted and screamed and told him that he could not take Matthew. I raged and fumed. I felt so broken at that moment that I didn't care about the consequences. And then I realized that God wanted me to wrestle my way *toward* him rather than *away from* him. God didn't squash me or reject me. He wasn't threatened by my pain or anger. Instead, he led me through the most incredible year of my life, which deepened my relationship with him. I don't believe that I would be serving God in the capacity I am today if I hadn't wrestled with him and found him trustworthy and good.

Going Deeper

Is Confrontation Appropriate?

We must start by asking the questions, *What is confrontation?* and *Is it appropriate?* For most men, their best friend in grade school was a boy they had a conflict with, bloodying each other's noses before resolving the conflict. It was this process of journeying through conflict that brought them to the point of being best friends. Many of us are afraid to wrestle with God, and that limits how deeply we will know him. It is important to keep the principle in mind: *the depth of our relationships will be determined by the level of conflict we are willing to journey through.*

Jacob and His "Gold Medal Match"

A biblical story that speaks clearly to this issue is the unique encounter between God and Jacob found in Genesis 32. Jacob is anticipating a deadly conflict with his older brother Esau, who years before had threatened to kill him because he had deceived their father in order to receive the blessing intended for Esau. Jacob did everything humanly possible to try to forestall Esau. He sent servants with gifts of livestock—goats, sheep, camels, cattle and donkeys—in waves ahead of him.

Throughout his life Jacob, had used trickery and deception to win, but this time he was at his wit's end. A man suddenly appears and Jacob wrestles with this man all night. Finally, at daybreak the man "touched the socket of Jacob's hip," wrenching his hip, and Jacob's eyes were opened to understand that his opponent was God. Jacob still holds on, however, realizing that only a blessing from God will save him.

It's important to point out that God changed Jacob. The name Jacob means "supplanter" or "deceiver"; but God transformed him and changed his name to Israel. The NIV text note on Gen 32:28 renders Israel "he struggles with God," and Strong's Concordance gives the meaning of Israel as "one who rules like God" or "Prince of God." It is clear from the three meanings of his new name that something happened that night that changed Jacob at a very deep level, at the level of his character. That change didn't happen until he wrestled with God. God allowed the struggle and, by means of it, transformed Jacob from a manipulating deceiver to one who rules with God's character.

What Keeps Us from Wrestling with God?

What are the barriers that keep us from wrestling with God? First, we're afraid that if we engage God at this intense, core level he will reject or judge us. Second, there are a lot of us, as church leaders, who equate wrestling with rebellion. Third, we fear that God is not good and we cannot trust him.

Each of us must ask the question, *Is there a specific area in my life that I am not willing to wrestle through with God?* I find that most men are afraid that God is going to squash or reject them, so they avoid engaging him. If we were absolutely certain at a heart level that God had good intentions for us, we would be a lot more likely to enter into this process and allow him to work in our lives. It is at this heart level, deep down in our gut, that many of us lack the conviction that God is truly good and therefore we can trust him. Our fear won't let us abandon ourselves to God and take the necessary leap of faith in order to experience transformation.

When Matthew was dying, I was broken enough that I didn't care about the consequences and I was willing to enter into this process. I believe that before Jacob wrestled with God he exhausted every possible avenue of escape. He fully expected to die the next day; his fear, or lack of trust in God, was no longer the issue. It seems that God must put us in life and death circumstances before we will wrestle with him. What would our lives be like if we didn't force God to allow such critical circumstances in order to engage him and struggle with him? How would our life and relationship with him change if we felt the freedom to regularly wrestle with him?

What is the Difference between Rebellion and Confrontation?

If we say that confronting God is not rebellion, then what is rebellion? Wrestling is struggling *toward* God and engaging him; rebellion is running *away from* God because we don't want to experience the pain of working through conflict. C. S. Lewis once said, "God whispers to us in our pleasures, speaks to us in our conscience, but shouts in our pains." Jacob had finally quit running from God.

As fathers, we don't like to have conflict with our children; but when we're wrestling with each other we're going to be changed by the struggle. God does not need to change. My relationship with him must change and grow. Do I want to become a spiritual patriarch or a spiritual dwarf?

I've heard church leaders say it's inappropriate for us to ever wrestle with God—it's a sign of irreverence toward him. They continue, "Why would we ever want to wrestle and question our God who loves us so much and has our best interests at heart?" For those of us who have not personally tested and experienced God at this level, this is the very place that we need to go in order to experience the character and love of God. Is this not part of the process of "working out our salvation with fear and trembling" that the apostle Paul calls us to in Philippians 2:12? Psalm 34:8 says, "Taste and see that the LORD is good." Wrestling with God is not disobedience, but rather, a place where we will find that he is good.

When Jacob wrestles with God it is the first time that he has engaged God at a level that will transform him. Before this event, Jacob was trying to make a deal with God. He interacted with God in the following pattern, "If you do this for me, I'll do this for you. If you bless me, I'll follow you." Self-focused dialogue falls away when he's wrestling with God. His actions say, "I'm hanging on to you. You're either going to have to kill me or give me a blessing and transform me." He is engaging God from a different perspective and at a deeper new level. Do you see the difference? We must come to the point where we understand that not only is wrestling not rebellion, but it ends our isolation from God.

The Critical Question

"Is God really good and can I trust him?" This could be one of the most important questions we ask concerning God. This is the crisis of trust in the Christian life that most of us slam up against. Without trust we cannot cross the barrier. In Job 38:3 God says to Job, "Brace yourself like a man; I will question you, and you shall answer me." What follows are four chapters of questions where God asks Job to correct his "worldly" perspective. The Lord's first question was, "Where were you when I laid the earth's foundation?" (Job 38:4). Finally, in chapter 42, Job is forced to respond. "I know that you can do all things; no plan of yours can be thwarted." In verse 5 Job describes the change in his relationship with God by saying, "My ears had heard of you but now my eyes have seen you." We, the men of the church, will not fully mature and become spiritual reproducers until we make this transition from just hearing about God to seeing him at work, testing and tasting that he is good.

We can't address this crisis of trust by ignoring that it's there or pretending that we should not wrestle with God. We must begin to engage God and challenge the men of our churches to engage him also. We must tell our stories of how God has changed us when we have wrestled with him. When I wrestled with God over Matthew's death, I found that he was good and I could trust him. I didn't feel warm and fuzzy. I was pushed to the point where my only option was to wrestle. And when I engaged him I found that he was good—the circumstances were not good, but he was! It is through wrestling that we will confirm God's goodness.

The Relational Diamond

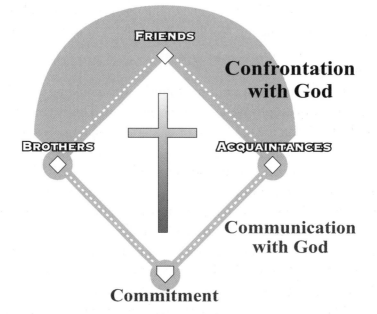

Let's look again at the Relational Diamond. It is journeying though conflict that moves us from being acquaintances to being friends. This principle is true in all of our relationships. Churches are full of people who are acquainted with God but they're not friends with him. They're not friends with God because they haven't trusted him enough to engage and test him to see and experience how "good" he really is. We're commanded to take this gigantic step: "taste and see how good he is" (Psalm 34:8). Do you see the importance of this process in our lives?

Growth in Reality

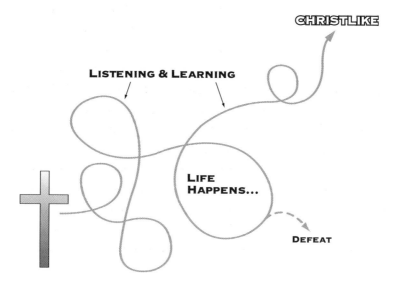

We shared this diagram with you earlier in the book. The downward loops of the lifeline illustrate the lifestyle of wrestling. It's essential we understand that we don't opt out of the process while we are wrestling. The only way we can fail is when we choose to opt out and are defeated.

Is Wrestling with God a One-time Event?

Wrestling with God is not something you do once and then you're done. I had open-heart surgery in 1999. There is no history of heart trouble in my family. Why did I end up with this? It was probably the result of stress in the spiritual battle. My immediate response was, "God, what are you doing? I've been serving you in full-time ministry for the last ten years. Why didn't you protect me?" Do you see what the crisis revealed in me? In 2002 I found out I had prostate cancer and I was right back in the battle again. Now, in each one of these circumstances God proved himself good and trustworthy. I am beginning to see that life will continually bring me back to wrestling with God.

"Know" God

Do you see the critical nature of this process? If we're not willing to communicate with God we can't go any deeper than minimal commitment. Only if we are willing to communicate and move into wrestling with God will we have the opportunity to know him intimately.

Let's shift our focus to what Paul said in Philippians 3:10: "I want to know Christ and the power of his resurrection and the fellowship of sharing in his sufferings, becoming like him in his death." Paul didn't say, "I want to know *about* Christ" or "I want to have *more information* about Christ." He said, "I want to *know* Christ." In the Old Testament, the word *know* is used to indicate the intimacy of sexual intercourse. We're not talking about "knowing" God at a surface level. Rather, this is knowing God at the most intimate level. If we will not trust and wrestle with God we cannot become spiritual fathers. It is through our intimate relationship with God that we can be used to reproduce this passionate, intimate relationship in others.

Are you missing the opportunity to know God at an intimate, deep level because you are unwilling or afraid to struggle toward him? Will you ...

1. **Get desperate** and run *to* God rather than *away from* him?
2. **Get brutally honest** and tell him the truth (which he already knows)?
3. **Give up control** and trust him?
4. **Hang on** and live moment by moment through faith?

If we can commit to God, then that allows us to communicate with him. If we will communicate and journey through conflict with God, we're at a point where we can begin to live in covenant relationship with him. *That covenant relationship allows us to co-labor or co-create with God.* These are the remaining topics before us.

Chapter 15

What is My Response to What Christ Has Done for Me?

The lost man and I could not be partners in the process of him being found until he could trust my wisdom, goodwill, and commitment to him. Many of us as Christian men have not come to the point of being fully "found" because we have not accepted and responded to God's commitment or covenant to us.

The Heart of the Message

After we have made a commitment to God and are communicating with him, we are able to work through conflict with him. Covenanting with God is the next step in the relational process. Our growing covenant relationship with God provides the foundation to serve him.

A covenant is an executed agreement determining how two or more parties will relate to each another. Grasping the opportunity to pursue God means I understand the commitment God has made to me as one of his children and I must respond to that knowledge and reality. For us to grow in our relationship with him, we must offer ourselves in service to him in response to his commitment to us and his great sacrifice on our behalf.

In doing this we are not instituting a new list of commandments, but rather verbalizing and executing our response to him. We have all made commitments to God, but many times they have been more in the vein of trying to obligate God to serve us rather than grasping the opportunity to serve him. Experiencing God's grace motivates us to live a life of gratitude rather than legalism.

What commitments have you made to God in the past? What commitments should you make now? In light of the principle of grasping the opportunity to live in relationship with God, can commitments be more of a negotiation than a covenant? *These questions must be answered in order to covenant with God. Your covenant is required before you can work alongside God or "co-labor" with him.*

Going Deeper

What is God Calling Us To?

In calling you to "covenant with God," you must understand that I'm not suggesting that God is calling you back to the legalistic Old Testament covenant. It is important for us as Christians to look at the eternal covenant God made with his people through Abraham, and understand how this covenant impacts us today.

Let's look at Genesis 15 where God executes his covenant with Abraham and his descendants. Abraham asks God how he can be certain that God's promises will come true. God directs Abraham to kill a number of animals and cut them in half. This is referred to as "cutting a covenant." We read in verse 17 that "a smoking firepot with a blazing torch"—a symbol of God's holy presence—"appeared and passed between the pieces." The significance of this action was that the executors of a covenant were to walk between the pieces of the slain animals, indicating the severe consequences of breaking their mutual covenant. God doesn't ask nor allow Abraham to walk between the halves of the animals, but he does so himself. If Abraham would have walked between the pieces of the slaughtered animals, the consequence for breaking the covenant would have been death. God was executing a one-sided covenant, a gracious covenant that would be fulfilled in its entirety by the death of his Son. Even today, through Christ, we are beneficiaries of this one-sided covenant.

One way to identify God's covenant with us is to list the promises given to believers in the New Testament. Then we must ask, *What is our reasonable response to those promises?* We often try to use our actions to manipulate God. If I respond to God by trying to manipulate him, I am trying to obligate him to give me what I want. By the nature of my response, I will reap the repercussions of obligation detailed in chapter 11— I will experience obligation, legalism, and slavery. God's promises are immutable because he does not change. His presence passed between the cut-up animals because he knew he would keep his covenant. *Our part is to respond properly to the covenant that God has provided.*

The Components of a Covenant Relationship with God

Entering into a covenant relationship with God has two main components. First, I must have an understanding of what God's promises are. Second, I have to see the importance of living in response to those promises. Covenanting with God means I agree to live in a way that demonstrates an appropriate response to what God has given me. There are numerous examples of covenant relationships within the Bible. Let's look at one of them.

In 1 Samuel, Hannah, the mother of Samuel, entered into a covenant with God before Samuel was born.

> Whenever the day came for Elkanah to sacrifice, he would give portions of the meat to his wife Peninnah and to all her sons and daughters. But to [his wife] Hannah he gave a double portion because he loved her, and the LORD had closed her womb. And because the LORD had closed her womb, her rival kept provoking her in order to irritate her. This went on year after year. Whenever Hannah went up to the house of the LORD, her rival provoked her till she wept and would not eat....
>
> Once when they had finished eating and drinking in Shiloh, Hannah stood up. Now Eli the priest was sitting on a chair by the doorpost of the LORD's temple. In bitterness of soul Hannah wept much and prayed to the LORD. And she made a vow, saying, "O LORD Almighty, if you will only look upon your servant's misery and remember me, and not forget your servant but give her a son, then I will give him to the LORD for all the days of his life, and no razor will ever be used on his head. (1 Samuel 1:4–7, 9–11)

Hannah did not try to manipulate God, but she appealed to her heavenly Father to meet her deepest need according to his grace. Her commitment was as firm as her faith, and she gave up her only son to God's service without reservation. This leads us to two vital questions: *What has God promised me?* and, *What is my reasonable response to his promises?*

God's Promises

Here are some of God's promises:

- *We have eternal life (John 3:36; 1 John 2:25).*
- *He will never leave or forsake us (Hebrews 13:5; Matthew 28:20).*
- *He will complete his work in us (Philippians 1:6).*
- *He will give us the Holy Spirit (John 14:16–17).*
- *We are his children and eternally loved (1 John 3:1–2).*
- *He forgives our sins (Colossians 2:13).*

We could continue to add pages and pages to this list. I encourage you to take a moment and write down some additional promises of God that come to your mind. When you're finished, ask yourself this question: *What is the appropriate response to each of these promises?*

God's Promises:	Our Response:
• We have eternal life.	Joy, thankfulness
• He will never leave nor forsake us.	Relief, security, love
• He will complete his work in us.	Confidence
• He will give us the Holy Spirit.	Empowered living
• We are his children and eternally loved.	Overwhelmed with delight
• He forgives our sins.	Thankfulness

Continue this pattern down through your list.

How difficult are the responses? Isn't it easy to respond to such wonderful promises? Look at the complete list—the six above plus your own. Which of these responses would be burdensome? You will have a hard time finding one response that is burdensome. Isn't that interesting? In the past, if you had called me to "covenant with God," I would have perceived that you were are asking me to commit to certain actions that obligated both God and me. In my heart I would be asking, "What is it that I have to do to get this from God?"

When I look back at my Christian life, I have walked through periods where I didn't sense or experience confidence. Was this because I didn't focus on God during the difficult struggles and didn't believe his promises? If I have tested God's character and I know that he's good and that I can trust him, then it is not a burden to respond to his promises and commitment with confidence. It is the only appropriate response to what God has done for me. I must continue to test him and see that he is good (Psalm 34:8).

I must keep focused on what God has promised—his covenant. My part of the covenant is to respond to what he's done. Yet, to be honest with you, I haven't lived most of my life in a way that's consistent with that understanding. For instance, I would say to myself, "I need to have my quiet time." Why? In essence, I was thinking that with correct behavior I could get the benefits of God's promises. God didn't say, "Dan, you need to have a quiet time—and if you don't, none of my promises are yours." I would be foolish not to spend time with him in communication, but it is not a prerequisite for receiving the benefits of his covenant.

The Encouragement of Brothers

Could it be that we need a constant reminder and encouragement from other men to live in response to the covenant? When I lack trust, I experience fear; and I need you to encourage me by reinforcing that God is good and he is never going to leave me. God promised that he's going to complete the good work that he began in me. I need brothers who remind me that the proper response to God's promises is to live the Christian life with confidence and boldness (Hebrews 10:24–25, 35).

Do you see how integral we are in supporting one another? Do you see why it's important that we understand what God's commitment to us is and that our commitment to him is only to respond? It's out of that response that we are able to reproduce. It is living in response to God and being empowered by his Spirit that provides the DNA of reproduction.

A Common and Dangerous Misunderstanding

Many of us, if we're honest, hold to the following belief: If I'm "good," I won't feel pain. I find it a lot easier to tell somebody else that this concept is wrong than to let go of this false thinking myself. Why is this? Do you struggle in the same way? I find that there is a deep-seated struggle in most of us. From the time we were small children we were taught, "If you're good, you'll be loved and you'll get what you want. If you're not good enough, you'll get punished."

Jesus' disciples demonstrated this belief when they asked Jesus who sinned and caused a man to be born blind. Jesus answered, "Neither this man nor his parents sinned, but this happened so that the work of God might be displayed in his life" (John 9:3). The disciples' question revealed the common misconception that if we are good we can avoid bad things. This misconception fights against and keeps us from accepting that God's promises are immutable. Yes, we should do good works—but in response to his promises, not in order to receive them.

The Trap of Not Believing God's Promises

I once heard a story that took place after Abraham Lincoln issued the Emancipation Proclamation. There were former slaves in the South who were still living in slavery. Someone walked up to a group of these former slaves and asked, "Have you not heard about Abraham Lincoln and the Proclamation?" Their response was, "We don't know nothing about no Abraham Lincoln." They'd been living in their lack of understanding, resulting in continued slavery.

A contrasting principle is illustrated in another story told of Lincoln. He was walking down the road and saw a young black girl on the auction block. Lincoln couldn't stand slavery, so he made the highest bid and got her off the auction block. As he began to walk away, she followed him. He explained to her, "You're free. Go on home." Her response was, "Thank you for my freedom. Now, would you please let me go home with you and serve you for the rest of my life."

These stories illustrate two truths: first, if you don't accept God's promises you don't get the benefits; second, many times the response to the gift of God's promises will bring us into the service of God. How many of us are still living in obligation—because we haven't fully accepted God's covenant of grace and truth?

This spiritual principle of covenant that we have been looking at is illustrated beautifully in the words of the hymn by Isaac Watts: "When I survey the wondrous cross, on which the Prince of glory died, my richest gain I count but lost, and pour contempt on all my pride. Were the whole realm of nature mine, that were a present far too small; love so amazing, so divine, demands my soul, my life, my all." A glad response to what the Lord has done for us is what he wants. Isn't that only fitting?

The Response of Worship

Worship is the proper response to such a great gift. Romans 12:1 tells us to "offer your bodies as living sacrifices, holy and pleasing to God—this is your spiritual act of worship." This Scripture reveals that the only appropriate response to what Christ has done for us is worship expressed through obedience. It sounds impossible to "offer your bodies as living sacrifices," but it is made easy when we realize we're not attempting to earn salvation. Worship as a living sacrifice is our response to the gift of salvation. Worship in response to Romans 12:1–2 is the mark of a man like Jacob, who wrestled with God, and, as a result, walked with a limp. A "limp" is evidence of changed character. I'll follow a man with a limp, but I won't follow a man who walks straight and tall but doesn't exhibit any evidence of wrestling with God and presenting himself as a living sacrifice. We must ask ourselves, *Are we going to be men who experience and expose our limps so that others can follow us?*

The Process

Think back to the foundation that has been laid throughout this book. In order to respond properly to God we must allow him to fill the father vacuum. As long as we see God through the lens of a deficient, earthly father we will never fully trust and follow him. We must be in a safe masculine place where we expose our wounds and allow our lives to be changed—a place where the Spirit of God and other men can speak into our lives. We need servant leaders—leaders who walk with a limp—to lead us through this process. Nothing, absolutely nothing, replaces the process of men coming together and journeying together. This is the only place where we accept the challenge, are called to battle, and become spiritual reproducers.

You will not participate in reproduction unless you're living the process. The process isn't living perfectly, but it is living with commitment and honesty. The only thing we're capable of doing is responding to his grace. If you're reading this book, more than likely you know that you are saved by grace. But deep down inside, most of us are pretty sure we're sanctified by works. Clearly, we must be convinced that we're not only saved by grace but also sanctified by grace.

Living out the covenant by responding to God's continued grace in our lives produces the foundation and DNA of reproduction. Reproduction is our calling and destiny. Reproduction builds us into spiritual fathers and is the process we're a part of as co-laborers and co-creators with Christ.

Part V

Pioneering the Pathway

Chapter 16

Are You Co-creating with God?

The lost man and I did not experience a long-term relationship. Our time together was too short to develop one. We were brought together by circumstances that allowed me to serve him to a point, but not beyond our initial contact. We needed commitment, trust, and continued contact in order to build bonds and experience the impact of a mature relationship.

Many of us are in a similar situation with God. We have a very limited and immature relationship with him, and yet, we wonder why it is so unsatisfying and why we see so few results. Only when we know God intimately can we co-labor with him. Only when we participate with him in the creation of spiritual life, as spiritual fathers, will we be truly satisfied and fulfilled.

The Heart of the Message

As men, we are on a search for significance. Almost from the day we are born we are trying to establish our value through what we do. We try to prove that we are worth something and that our lives and existence are significant. Sports, work, positions, accomplishments, conquests, and our addictive behaviors are some of the mechanisms we use to try to prove that we have worth. We want to create something that will last. Every man lives in fear that he will come to the end of his life and look back and see that it counted for nothing.

When we are younger this desire for significance is not on the surface, but it is there—deep down inside of us. As young men we may not even know what is driving us; but as we approach middle age our search for significance will become more obvious. At midlife many men find themselves at one of two points. They have either accomplished what they set out to do and they find themselves asking, "Is that all there is?" or they realize they are never going to reach the goals they set for themselves. The first leads to a midlife crisis and the second leads to despair. What is the alternative?

As we have seen earlier, God has called his men to mature in relationship with him until they become spiritual reproducers or spiritual fathers. It is this legacy that brings the satisfaction and significance we hunger for.

In 2001 I was invited to Germany to speak at a men's conference. I was asked to speak on the subject of the father vacuum. In the process I saw the tremendous need in Europe for spiritual fathers. As I spoke to and prayed with men and women concerning this important issue, God began to deal with me in a very unusual way. He brought men and women into relationship with me who began to see me as a spiritual father. I was at the airport leaving when I called one of the men whom I had been ministering with a "brother," and he stopped me and told me that I was more of a "father" to him. I was uncomfortable with that and later in our conversation I called him a "brother" a second time. Again he stopped me and said that I was more of a "father" to him.

When I got on the plane God began to deal with me concerning the opportunities I had missed to be a spiritual father because I had not even seen the possibility or the responsibility and privilege of being one. I had been so fixated on establishing my worth through what I did in "the ministry" that I had missed the opportunity to be a man who could leave an eternal legacy by participating with God in the creation of spiritual life. Over the next few months, I saw men and women healed and growing as they experienced the love and acceptance of a spiritual father.

Do you feel a need for that kind of significance? Do you want to leave a legacy that will last for eternity? Are you willing to progress through a relationship with God from being a spiritual child to becoming a spiritual father who reproduces spiritual children who are becoming spiritual reproducers? As we've learned from 1 John 2:12–14, your spiritual children need to mature through (1) having their sins forgiven and beginning to know the Father; (2) to becoming spiritual young men who have the Word of God in them and are overcoming the evil one; (3) to becoming spiritual fathers who are beginning to know God intimately, in his completeness, and are themselves reproducing spiritual children.

Going Deeper

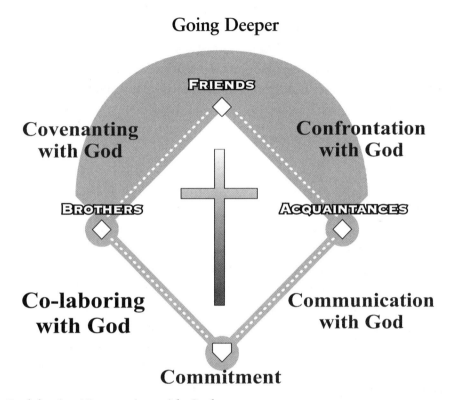

Co-laboring/Co-creating with God

When we understand the meaning of covenanting with God and are beginning to live in covenant relationship, we are able to co-labor with him. It's not out of my will as a man that I'm going to be a spiritual reproducer or a father, but it's out of my willingness to allow God to accomplish his promises through me and transform me so that I can be used in reproduction. Let's take a quick look at what we mean by co-laboring/co-creating with God.

Every healthy relationship produces something. In a marriage it may be children and a lasting impact on the community. In a business it may be a product and income for those who are employed at that business. As a general rule, healthy relationships produce a product that is positive for everyone in the relationship.

When we are in relationship with God, the product of our relationship is that we are given the privilege of participating with him in creation by co-laboring. Co-laboring is the opportunity we have to be a part of what God is doing. As we have said before, many of us are caught in the trap of trying to *do* things for God. God does not need us to do anything for him, but he does want us to join him in what he is doing.

When God formed us physically, and again when he redeemed us, he gave us certain gifts. We have the opportunity to offer those gifts back to him in relationship and use them to establish his kingdom wherever we are. As we saw in the last chapter on covenanting, God has given us so much when he extended grace to us that the only reasonable response is a life of gratitude lived out for him. What are the gifts that you have been given, that in response to your relationship to him, you can now offer back to him to be used in the process of co-laboring or co-creating with him?

List your gifts, abilities and resources. Then, list the places where you see God at work around you. Lastly, list the issues and causes that you are passionate about. The things you are passionate about often help identify where God is calling you. The foundational and universal calling in our lives is the passionate pursuit of God. That passion to know God and be known by him is the primary characteristic that should be reproduced in others. How can you use your gifts, resources and passion to serve God where he is working?

Leaving a Lasting Legacy

We started this chapter by looking at every man's desire for significance and we need to end by focusing on that desire and its fulfillment in leaving a legacy. God's first command to mankind in Genesis 1:28 and Christ's last command on earth in Matthew 28:18–20 make it clear that we are to reproduce. But what is it that we are to reproduce? We are to reproduce the pursuit of God.

The last section of this book has been focused on the passionate pursuit of God. It is that pursuit that the apostle Paul articulates in Philippians 3:10. He identifies three results of an intimate relationship with Christ: the power of his resurrection, the fellowship of his suffering, and the transforming power of his presence. Another perspective of this pursuit is communicated in 1 John 2:12–14. John identifies the characteristics of the spiritual father as one who intimately knows God as the eternal "I AM" and is reproducing that pursuit into coming generations of spiritual children who in turn become spiritual mothers and fathers. Our pursuit of Christ prepares us and allows us to become spiritual reproducers. We cannot be used to reproduce what we do not possess. It is only when we become spiritual reproducers that we are spiritual fathers and can leave a lasting, eternal legacy.

If you haven't already begun the pursuit, would you join with a band of brothers who are pursuing God together? This is your spiritual destiny. Men pursuing God on a spiritual pathway within the church is the very thing needed to restore the church to its calling of building spiritual fathers. My personal mission, and our mission at Building Brothers is to serve the local church in discovering its pathway to continually reproducing spiritual fathers.

Chapter 17

What is the Next Step?

After the lost man left me, it likely took him the rest of the day to reach his camp by walking trails that he had already walked. The question that remains is, *How did he respond the next morning?* Was he a prisoner in his own camp, afraid to venture beyond sight of his camp? Did he get out maps and process through where he had been the previous day so that he understood the terrain? Or did he stay glued to a hunting partner who knew the area better than he did? I will never know, but what is clear is that his response to this experience was going to determine how effectively he would accomplish his goal of hunting. His willingness and commitment to grow was going to lead him either to freedom or bondage.

In similar fashion, we may see the crisis in the church and the goal of pursuing God in order to become spiritual fathers. But if we are not willing to walk trails that we have not walked before, we cannot address the crisis. What is the pathway that will lead us out of the wilderness?

How Can We Meet the Crisis in the Church and the Culture?

Throughout this book, we have seen the church's failure to embrace God's mission for the church as communicated in Ephesians 4:11–13. The Ephesians 4 church will demonstrate unity, maturity and Christlikeness. Looking at that passage in light of the call to be repro-ducers in Matthew 28:18–20, we find that the church's primary role is to help men and women mature into spiritual fathers and mothers, reproducing future spiritual fathers and mothers. The church is in a crisis brought on by not fulfilling its primary calling. It defeats itself and stops short of being salt and light, the preserver and corrector of the culture. As the church fails in its reproductive role, our culture is left in crisis and continues to slide into relativism, self-focus and moral decline.

If you agree that the culture and the church are in crisis, then it is important to ask key questions so that we can begin to address this crisis.

Can we heal the crisis in the culture without healthy families?

Can we have healthy families without men who are spiritual fathers?

Is the church the place to build spiritual fathers?

Are pastors, elders, and leaders living as spiritual fathers—which is essential to the reproduction of spiritual fathers?

How do we help pastors and leaders become reproducing spiritual fathers?

Healthy families are the building blocks of the culture and the church, but how can we build healthy families without first building spiritual fathers?

In my spiritual journey in the church during the last half-century, I was challenged to know the Word, fight the spiritual battle, and become a spiritual young man, but I was not challenged to become a reproductive spiritual father (see 1 John 2:12–14). If we are going to address and solve the current crisis, we must start by calling our churches back to the mission of the church as laid out in Ephesians 4:11–13. We must also become leaders who stand ready and committed to carry out our God-given role of bringing God's people to maturity so that they can then carry out their mission of reproducing passionate followers of Christ. In order to accomplish this we must have a pathway that is a process of taking men from immaturity to maturity—from spiritual childhood to spiritual fatherhood.

The Pathway

The pathway must be **visible** so that every man in the church can see and understand the call. It must be **definable** so that the process is understandable and not hidden or mysterious to the men in the church. It must be **joinable** so that each man can be a part of the process. Even if the pathway is visible and definable, it is useless if men cannot be a part of it. It must also be **normative** so that every man in the church knows that this is the church's pathway to prepare each man to participate in the mission of his church. The pathway will never be considered the norm for the church if the church's functional leaders are not part of the process and are not calling the men of the church to join them.

It is clear that the male leaders of the church are the key to meeting the current crisis. The critical questions are these:

- **Are we as leaders willing to become mature spiritual fathers who the men of our church can follow?**
- **Are we willing to understand the journey God has taken us on and create a pathway inviting the men of the church to journey with us into the passionate pursuit of God and to reproduce that pursuit in others?**

Building this pathway starts with the functional leaders of the church pioneering the journey by coming together in relationship and intentionally breaking down the universal barriers that are keeping them from pursuing God. Building Brothers is a ministry founded and committed to helping church leaders journey through this process. The universal barriers that must be broken down are as follows:

The father vacuum must be filled by God in order for men to see God as he is and pursue him.

We must *experience and create a masculine context* in the church that allows a man to come home and be safe.

Men must *become servant leaders* who produce unity and trust so that they can lead the church into the pursuit of God.

We must *grasp the opportunity* to experience an intimate relationship with our Lord and *pursue God.*

Building Brothers offers a year-long, interactive process for leaders to break down these barriers and discover their congregation's unique pathway to build men into mature spiritual fathers. *Warning:* If the process is administered as a program rather than an ongoing life journey, it will fail.

What Needs to Happen?

- There must be a consensus among the leaders that the building of men into mature leaders is foundational to the church.
- These leaders must be willing to pioneer the process. Under the guidance of and with the participation of the senior pastor, these pioneers must become what they want their men to become. This is an extended lifestyle process, not an event or program.
- These pioneers must understand their journey, break down the barriers that keep men from pursuing God and identify the pathway that God is revealing to them. When the plan is clear, it is time to invite the men of the church to taste what the leaders are experiencing and join them in the process.
- The pathway and plan should continually be fine-tuned by asking the question, *What is keeping our men from pursuing God?* Focus on the answers, and help men remove the barriers.

Programs or Reproduction

For the last fifty years the American Church has been searching for the "magic bullet" in the form of the right program or event that will bring about the transformation of God's people into mature reproducers of the faith. Yet, we continue to see the church shrink in numbers and in its influence upon the culture. Could the expectation that a *program* will accomplish this primary mission of the church actually be a primary barrier to the effectiveness of the church? Could it be that we as leaders must overcome the "program mentality" within the church if we are to move back to significance and life?

What is the difference between a program (or production method) and a reproductive process? Programs focus on behavioral issues, or the *doing*. Reproductive processes focus on the transformational changes that must take place to *become* like Christ. Christian tools or resources are typically looked at as the "key" to bringing about the result we desire. (Haven't we all thought, at one point, that if we could just find the "right" resource then people would be changed?) As leaders it is imperative to ask the question: Do you ever get a reproduction result from a production method?

In reproduction, the *process* is the instrument that the Spirit of God uses to pass on his DNA. The reproductive process creates an environment where the Spirit is encouraged and free to work in our hearts. Programs can be used as an element of the process but cannot by themselves bring about transformation. The New Testament clearly indicates that the Holy Spirit brings about change and transformation in God's people. When we expect the tool or program to bring about change, aren't we displacing the Spirit from his proper place and in essence setting up the program as an idol?

When Moses was on the mountain receiving the Ten Commandments from God, the children of Israel exhibited a similar response when they asked Aaron to make "gods who will go before us" (Exodus 32:1), resulting in Aaron fashioning the golden calf. They didn't like the process and relational model that God had set up. They wanted a God who would allow them to control the results. Aren't we doing the same thing when we depend on tools and programs to find a quick and manageable shortcut?

Christ modeled a radically different approach as he prepared the twelve disciples to build his church. Jesus reproduced his passion and heart in them as they walked and lived together over three years. However, they were not effective reproducers until they were empowered by the Spirit at Pentecost. How can we follow this lifestyle model that Christ so clearly gave us?

We model Christ's leadership when we *become* the firstfruits and *then* reproduce this into the men in the church. Through this model the church can restore the reproductive, intergenerational model of the first-century church, establishing a pathway to take men from immaturity to maturity. Men must be introduced to the saving power of Christ so that they become *spiritual children*. They must be matured by the Word of God until the Word is in them and they effectively become warriors, or *spiritual young men*. Finally, they must be challenged and encouraged to know God intimately, beginning to know him in his entirety, and to be used as *spiritual fathers* to reproduce the next generations of *spiritual fathers*. It is only through a reproductive process inherent in the pathway that the church will return to health.

We stand at a crossroad. Will we continue to put our hope and efforts into the next "bigger and better" program? Will we continue to search for the magic bullet that will transform the church and bring God's people to maturity in a short period of time? Or will we begin to pursue an intimate relationship with God and invite others onto that maturing pathway with us? The stakes are high. Don't miss this opportunity.

Institutionalization

One of the traps that keeps us focused on programs rather than a life-changing reproductive process is the pressure and movement toward institutionalization. Only as we understand and focus on the *mission* will we be able to evaluate the effectiveness of our efforts in the church.

When the mission is not clear, we will gravitate toward programs with measurable outcomes. Programs assume that the method is the mission and that the method brings about the desired result.

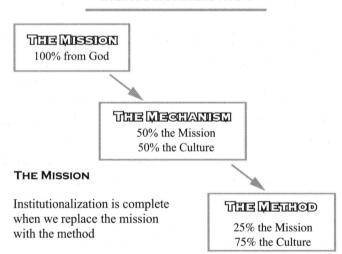

INSTITUTIONALIZATION

THE MISSION
100% from God

THE MECHANISM
50% the Mission
50% the Culture

THE MISSION

Institutionalization is complete when we replace the mission with the method

THE METHOD
25% the Mission
75% the Culture

One of the stories that I like to use to illustrate this principle is the beginning of the traditional Sunday night service. In the 1880s, gaslights became available and the church saw a tremendous opportunity for evangelization. If they would just install gaslights and turn them on they would draw a crowd and they could share the gospel with that crowd of unbelievers. Look with me as we apply the progression illustrated in the diagram above. The *mission* was the Great Commission to go and preach the gospel, making disciples. The *mechanism* was the church. And the *method* was the Sunday night gaslit service. Now let's move forward seventy years to the 1950s. For many years almost every church had a Sunday night service. In time that became one of the marks used to judge a church's spirituality. The primary mission of preaching the gospel was lost. The original *mission*, the Great Commission, had been replaced by the *method*, the Sunday night service.

It is incredibly easy to slide into replacing the *mission* with the *method*, or program, that we are using. If we execute the program flawlessly, we still are only able to accomplish at most a fraction of the mission. The temptation to replace God's mission with our method is almost irresistible. If we allow the method to become the mission, the mission is lost and we are left searching for the next "perfect program" or magic bullet.

Importance of Pastors, Elders, and Leaders

Let's go back to the beginning issue in this chapter. If the crisis in the church is to be met, the men of the church—through reproduction— must be brought to maturity as spiritual fathers. Pastors, elders, and leaders: *You may not be the problem, but you are definitely part of the solution.* Only *you* can identify the importance of building God's people to maturity so that they can become spiritual mothers and fathers. Only *you* can begin to model and call the men of the church to the process. Only *you* can keep the church on its mission by calling the people back to God's mission. You must become the pioneers and firstfruits of the reproductive process.

Dream with me now: What would it look like to begin to change the culture of the church into a reproductive culture focused on bringing men and women to maturity? The change must start with the male leaders of the church affirming the mission of the church and the essential role that mature spiritual fathers play in the culture of the church. Can we maintain an effective intergenerational ministry without embracing a reproductive church model?

Turn to chapter 18 and let me help you understand what the final steps are to embracing this process.

Chapter 18

The Impact of the process

Do You Want to Be a Spiritual Grandfather?

Through these past years God has brought many men into my life and given me the opportunity to build into their lives. During my trip to Germany in 2001, which I've shared about in this book, God revealed that the process of discipling was really better termed *spiritual fathering*. I was partnering with Rainer, a men's ministry leader in Germany, when he began to tell me I was becoming a spiritual father to him. His using the term "spiritual father" in describing me made me feel very uncomfortable. He refused to back down and repeatedly told me that God was using me as a father in his life. This Germany trip was the time when God put many pieces in place to understand this idea of spiritual fathering.

During this same trip throughout Germany I spoke extensively on the father vacuum issue that is so prevalent in men's lives. The father vacuum is the hole inside of us, caused by deficiencies in our relationship with our earthly father that significantly impacts the way we see and relate to God. I was helping men begin the healing process by providing an opportunity for them to experience the blessing of God their Father through the spoken word of godly men into their lives.

I was invited to speak at many smaller gatherings where a young German woman, Nikola, was my interpreter. After a few days of this I began to perceive the difficult position this was putting her in. I had found out that she had never known her father, and yet I was having her translate words about the father vacuum and prayers of blessing for others. As we were leaving a Full Gospel Business Men's meeting, I asked her if she wanted God's blessing spoken to her. She immediately answered, "Of course," as if she'd been patiently waiting for me to *finally* ask this question!

That blessing, an act of spiritual fathering, changed her life—and mine as well. Long distance, I walked with her until God provided Rainer and his wife, Sibylle, as spiritual parents for her and I then became, in essence, her spiritual grandfather. Since that time I've had the opportunity to preach at Nikola's wedding, where she married a wonderful young man, Gionatan; and I've continued in an ongoing spiritual fathering/grandfathering relationship with both of them.

It has been powerful, yet humbling, to see God using me in his process of spiritual reproduction and the ongoing generational impact. I have repeatedly experienced God confirming the awesome power of this message: calling his men to become spiritual fathers, and through this calling, leaving a spiritual legacy while experiencing the eternal significance we as men long for.

Now I'd like to take you beyond my experience by having you read a couple of stories that poignantly illustrate the process of spiritual fathering and reproduction.

Rick's Story
Written by Rick Ellsmore
Building Brothers Staff

I sat anxiously waiting to talk to Dan Schaffer as the thunder of male voices and the clatter of forks on plates swirled around me. Dan and I had spoken multiple times on the phone but had never met face-to-face. *What would he think of me? Would he see weakness in my eyes? Would the personal struggles in my spiritual journey rebuff him or would he be the man to help me take further steps in my adventure with Christ?*

My mind was drawn back to the amazing expedition the Spirit had initialized in my soul. It had been over three years since Christ had resurrected a disconnected and desperate man—a man who lived in shame and self-deprivation, estranged from his wife and all others in his life. I had lived on a lonely island due to the intense level of fear that I would be "found out" and be seen as the man I believed myself to be: "unlovable"—even by God.

A snapshot of this amazing redemptive process came into focus: my Father-God provided a *spiritual father* to guide me and walk beside me—Merle Engle. I remembered stepping into the warmth of his home for the first time and being so scared of his rejection that my mouth couldn't get out the words that flooded my mind. Hesitantly, I started to spit out the putrid content of these deeply embedded wounds and give voice to my feelings of desperation. Merle cried with me. He prayed with me. He gave me a lasting hug that hasn't ended in the eight years since then. Ultimately, he showed me the grace my heart had longed for in another man. That day was the beginning of Merle Engle becoming a vital part of the very fabric of my soul.

I thought about the eclectic collection of "tools," other spiritual mentors, whom Christ used in performing the "heart surgery" so needed in my life—Gray LeMaster, John Kriz, Mark Schatzman and Kevin Huff. Each of these warriors chose to walk alongside me in my "dark night of the soul." They saw all my ugly and bleeding wounds, yet still desired to play a part in helping them heal into scars to be used for God's glory.

Finally, Dan sat down beside me—and we immediately connected on a deep spiritual level. I knew within five minutes that this would be the man who would walk alongside me on the next leg of my journey. I talked; he listened. I cracked the door on my sinful and wounding choices; he modeled grace, wisdom and acceptance. The process of my spiritual maturing was about to speed up significantly!

I had experienced a spiritual father in my life but I longed to walk with a man who could put flesh over the skeleton in this process of spiritual transformation. I was interacting with the desperately wounded men God was placing in my life, but Dan brought clarity by opening my eyes to the tremendous need in the church and culture at large. This message had been entrusted to him at Building Brothers, and it was time to walk alongside of him to cull out the wisdom and experience I needed in order to leap forward in my own journey with Christ.

My family and I moved to Colorado and joined in the battle. Dan and the team, Ken Moldenhauer and Dan'l Hollis, became my brothers through the continued peaks and valleys of growth on this winding path. As we "did life together" (and that sure is messy), an amazing process was set in motion—a life's message began to explode within me.

This has played out in some truly astounding ways. First, in my desire for an authentic relationship with Jesus that now drives my life! This desire has propelled me to be as real and authentic as I can be with wounded men in my life. Second, in loving my wife Gretchen—my beauty, my soul mate! Because my Father God has had me in a process of healing my own wounding, I have been able to play an important role in Christ healing the wounds in her soul. Third, in being able to love my three boys, Erik, Mitchell and Jake, on a genuine level and break the generational wounding that is part of my heritage. Finally, I've been able to walk with men as a spiritual father—showing them an aggressive grace that infiltrates their souls, giving them a hope and vision of being able to reproduce their healing and the life of Christ in other men.

In the last six months, I have personally owned this life-changing message of building a pathway toward becoming spiritual transformers and reproducers. I go to sleep with this on my mind and I wake up dreaming about it. My desire has become to walk alongside men and help them: (1) see that they are sons of the Royal King; (2) discover that they carry a father vacuum wound (at some level) and are in need of healing and redemption; (3) realize that they have a God-given hunger to live out a godly masculinity; and (4) understand that God has specifically made them to lead their family and church community into a deeper relationship with God and each other and their culture to experience Jesus Christ!

I came to Building Brothers not fully understanding the process that must happen for this revolution to take place in my heart—and in the hearts of all men. I came not fully understanding the concept of "dying to self" that must happen in order for the Spirit of God to resurrect our spiritual passions and purpose. I came not fully understanding how significantly wounded and disconnected most men are from their earthly father, which ultimately shackles the depth of their relationship with their heavenly Father. I now understand the process that Jesus and his disciples modeled that must be birthed in each one of us in order to impact and change the hearts of men—and God's bride, his church!

Pastor Ricci's Story
Written by Pastor Ricci Arthur
Senior Pastor, Dresden, Ohio United Methodist Church

I first heard Dan Schaffer speak in 2002 at a men's rally within my denomination. I remember going up to him and saying, "You've just described my life! I've dealt with a huge father vacuum. I reconciled with my dad before he died and received his blessing, so this issue of the father's blessing is the journey I've personally been traveling."

I attended the Building Brothers Leadership Training in August of 2003, along with about twenty other pastors and leaders from around the country. I arrived with high expectations—and frankly, the experience *exceeded* them! I found the interaction of the men to be tremendous. There is just something awesome about men sharing from their hearts, with all the laughter and tears that comes with it. That is from God! I grew tremendously from this depth of interaction.

I learned so much from Dan and the Building Brothers team, especially in the way the training was handled. First of all, the questions were open-ended. Dan would pause and look at us silently, allowing us time to process; and *then* we were asked to respond. That was incredible—it made the material our own! Second, Dan's vulnerability at various points was wonderful. He never had the attitude, "Look at all I know. I have arrived; follow me." It was great to learn more about the process other men had personally experienced and lived out.

I quickly realized that I couldn't handle the entire process of trans-forming men in my church alone, so I turned to a brother in my church. It was apparent that he had an appetite for service and growth in his spiritual maturity and a desire to get more deeply involved in the lives of others. I started the process of pouring my life into his life on a weekly basis. There was incredible transformation as we "did life together" and started dialoguing through the Building Brothers materials. I built into him and he took over the leadership of the Building Brothers process.

I discovered that Building Brothers is a process of discipleship in which you get in touch with the wounds of your past so you can be a disciple of Christ in the present with other men of like mind. To carry out this discovering at a heart level we needed to get our men away from the normal stresses and distractions of life. So the decision was made to facilitate the Building Brothers process by using the videos as the guide for a weekend retreat. Our Phase I retreat drew a significant number of men. I remember a poignant moment when Dan, via the video, asked this question: "Have you ever had a time when your earthly father said, 'I love you'?" Seventy-five percent said this had *never* happened. These wounds are the elephant in the living room that everybody in the church is ignoring. I continue to hear the question, "Why don't men get more involved?" I believe it's because we as leaders within the church are not specifically addressing these wounds.

Amazingly, almost every man that attended this retreat has chosen to either be involved with Building Brothers or serve the church in some other form. This was a pivotal weekend in the life of our church!

I have personally experienced that most pastors don't realize that discipleship is the key. As pastors, we tend to focus more on "Bible studies" than on "intentional discipleship"—which is about forming us to become more like Christ, using the Bible as the guide. It's important that we know God's Word, but so often in typical Bible studies we tend to lose the character development and healing in the midst of the study. That's the power of the Building Brothers process: it assists in putting the pieces in place to allow men to go deeper into relationship with Christ first, and with other men secondly.

I see my role as more of a grandfather to this process within my church. I am to be a spark plug in coming up with an intentional plan to reach the men in our church. Also, I am to be like a bulldog with my leaders, continually asking them the question, "What are we doing to help the people in our small groups become more like Christ?" I'm realizing just how countercultural this is in the life of the modern church; people look at me as if I'm from outer space when I use this language.

Building Brothers has become a part of the fabric of my personal ministry with men and within our church. I thank them for being willing vessels to serve me and the men of my church!

Pastor Chip's Story
Written by Pastor Clyde "Chip" Hinds
Senior Pastor, Wister, Oklahoma, Church of God (Seventh Day)

Most Christian congregations in America are significantly lacking "something". I believe that "something" is a pathway for men—beginning with a place for them to come to know Christ in a comfortable setting and continuing with a track within the church that would lead them to maturity in Christ, reproducing mature Christians over and over again.

I remember first hearing of Building Brothers and thinking, "Is this just another program to fire up my men? Why will this be different?" Through the years I had witnessed my men participate in large events and get pumped up but yet only days later fall right back into their comfortable rut. I heard Dan give an overview of the "process" and immediately understood that Building Brothers was going to be different.

I decided to find a man within our congregation who had a heart for building men within our church. I asked Lamar Ford to attend the Building Brothers Leadership Training with me, and together we experienced the benefit of training men in this process. In my past years of ministry there had been a sense of hopelessness in reaching men. *Building Brothers Leadership Training helped me realize that reaching men is not hopeless. I walked away saying, "I can do this as a leader of these men! We can do this as a church!"*

Attending the Leadership Training helped me to personally engage my heavenly Father at an even deeper level. This didn't, or couldn't, happen until I took a more intense look at the whole father vacuum concept and the painful relationships surrounding this issue for me. You see, my parents divorced when I was only a year old. When I was twelve years old, my father stated, "You are none of mine."

I thought I was completely over this wounding, but realized more of the healing process and a deepened trust in God needed to take place in my life. It wasn't until this training that I understood *why* I was beginning to learn to trust my heavenly Father. I was subconsciously saying, "I hope God won't be like my earthly father and abandon me when I need him." Well, my heavenly Father is not like my earthly father. These three days allowed both Lamar and I to accelerate through some of these large issues surrounding our fathers.

As a pastor, I needed to tap into Lamar's spiritual hunger and heart for men, so I empowered him to take the leadership of the men in our church. I realized that I didn't have the time or energy to "be the man" to drive this process. Rather, I needed to have a vision to personally build into the men who can steer this vehicle—usually not the most popular individuals, or even the most gifted, but the ones who have a calling on their lives to serve. As pastors, we are to *teach, trust and turn 'em loose!*

Lamar and I have shared this hope with the men in our church, and they have quickly caught it! We have seen these men dealing with issues that have kept them from a richer relationship with Jesus Christ. One brother in my group shared, "You are the men I'm close to, the ones I depend upon in my spiritual walk. When I need help, this is where I come!"

We've established these close and personal relationships and have developed resources for these men in the spiritual battles that take place in their lives. This has generated a desire to see other men experience what they have experienced. Even though we are only six months into this process, they are already engaging other men. Reproduction is already taking place!

We are having men visit our church and *they are staying.* One of these men recently said to me, "This church is taking me faster than I'm comfortable going, but I don't know how I can say no to God." He's pumped about the opportunity to get involved in the second year of Building Brothers.

I strongly encourage pastors to attend the Leadership Training—but not alone. Bring a man, or a few men, with you who have this hunger I've spoken about. Having Lamar with me helped me to walk away and see the vision be borne out six months later. It was as if I had a Building Brothers staff member right in my church.

This movement of men within our church has been a pathway that launches men further in their spiritual growth so they can engage Christ on a much deeper level. I have seen them grow into spiritually mature and Christ-centered disciples. We need to lead the way, helping them become *believers building believers* (we've added this to our church sign!).

I've heard Lamar say, "In order to reach men we must establish a comfortable place so they will take the 'earplugs' out and really listen to us. It's only then that we can properly deal with their earthly father issues and ultimately their issues with their heavenly Father. The coloration between the two can't be ignored any longer! In these 'travels of the heart' they are brought to a place of experiencing the holiness of God, which compels them to repent and move forward spiritually." In establishing this pathway, we have assisted our men in running the spiritual race that Christ has called them, and us, to run!

I praise God for the men of Building Brothers who have taught us to bring out the "something" in our church; they've come up with a viable solution to the crisis within the church. I thank them for their generous expenditures of time and energies in assisting us in becoming all that God intended for us to be in Christ. We are still in the process, but the evidence of improvement is already being experienced; the vision of what we can become is coming into focus.

Building Brothers Leadership Training

The Building Brothers Leadership Training is intended to help a church core leadership team of at least two to five men have a mini-experience of the Building Brothers process. Over an intensive three-day period these leaders will be exposed to the four phases of this process. Here is an overview of what they will experience:

- Learn to create a safe masculine environment and overcome common obstacles that keep men from pursuing God.
- Discover Christ's model of servant leadership where men are taught to be leaders who build trust and unity.
- Grasp the vital nature of defining a unique pathway for their men to spiritually mature.
- Understand how to call and encourage their men to become spiritual fathers who are building into other men, reproducing men who themselves are becoming spiritual fathers.

The Building Brothers Leadership Training is also aimed at helping the attending pastors and leaders begin to experience some personal life transformations; overcome obstacles that prevent them from personally pursuing God; understand how to build a unique pathway for their men to spiritually mature and grow and learn how to become spiritual fathers themselves.

Because an intention of the Leadership Training is to model a safe masculine environment for men, the format of the training is a dynamic mixture of honest, interactive discussion; impacting teachings and presentations; confidential sharing and disclosure of personal experiences; hands-on interaction within each of the phases; men engaging each other around real issues and experiences of personal transformation.

Each man who completes the Building Brothers Leadership Training will be prepared to lead or participate in a core group of men within their church who are committed to entering into the life-changing, year-long Building Brothers four-phase process.

Building Brothers is committed to supporting local churches through this reproductive process and provides congregations with the necessary support materials:

- Building Brothers *Leadership Training*
- Building Brothers *Four-Phase Process Video/DVD Series*
- Building Brothers *Leaders Guide*
- Building Brothers *Field Manuals*
- Building Brothers *Facilitation Assistance*

What's Your Next Step?

Where are you in this process we've laid out? Where are the men of your church in the process? Lost in the woods, asking for help, finding the way back, or maybe taking the beginning steps? Let me challenge you to begin to go before God and prayerfully listen for his direction concerning the issues we've raised in this book. Do you see the need for a change in the culture of the church—making it a place of safety and trust where men are becoming spiritual fathers who reproduce additional spiritual fathers through a defined pathway? If so, let me suggest the following plan of action:

- Gather a core leadership team of at least two to five men who will commit to the Building Brothers Leadership Training.
- Register and attend the Building Brothers Leadership Training. Please visit our website at www.buildingbrothers.org so you can register and gather the complete details.

Building Brothers is committed to walking alongside you and your church in the battle that is taking place for the hearts of men!

About the Author

Dan Schaffer is the founder and president of Building Brothers. He has a deep, spiritual passion for building men and has been a spiritual father to men for over thirty years. Dan was one of the four men who founded Promise Keepers. His love for the outdoors often finds him hunting and fishing in the Colorado Rockies. Dan and his wife, Jan, live in Littleton, Colorado, and have two grown children.